A Jenny

My Life Electric

Jenny Webb

Matt Cresswell

Copyright © 2021 Jenny Webb
and Matt Cresswell

All rights reserved

ISBN: 9798479812798

The day must come when electricity will be for everyone, as the waters of the rivers and the wind of heaven. It should not merely be supplied, but lavished, that men may use it at their will. In towns it will flow as the very blood of society. Every home will tap abundant power, heat and light, like drawing water from a spring. And at night it will light another sun in the dark sky, putting eternal warmth that will return to the old world, melting even the highest snow.

Emile Zola

They thought I'd be rubbish because I'm "only a woman". But I thought: "I'll have you."

Jenny Webb

CONTENTS

1   Editor's Introduction   1

2   Saturday, 26 August 1972   3

3   Jenny Arrives   5

4   The Bombs Fall   13

5   A London Childhood   33

6   Powering On   56

7   Our Woman in Russia   79

8   Friday, 7 July 1978   96

9   The Cooking Revolution   97

10   My Million-Seller   107

11   The Face of the Electricity Industry   114

12   By Royal Request   131

13   The End of an Era   137

14   Saturday, 29 October 1994   141

15   An Old Lady and her Suitcase   142

16   Afterword   173

17   Bibliography   177

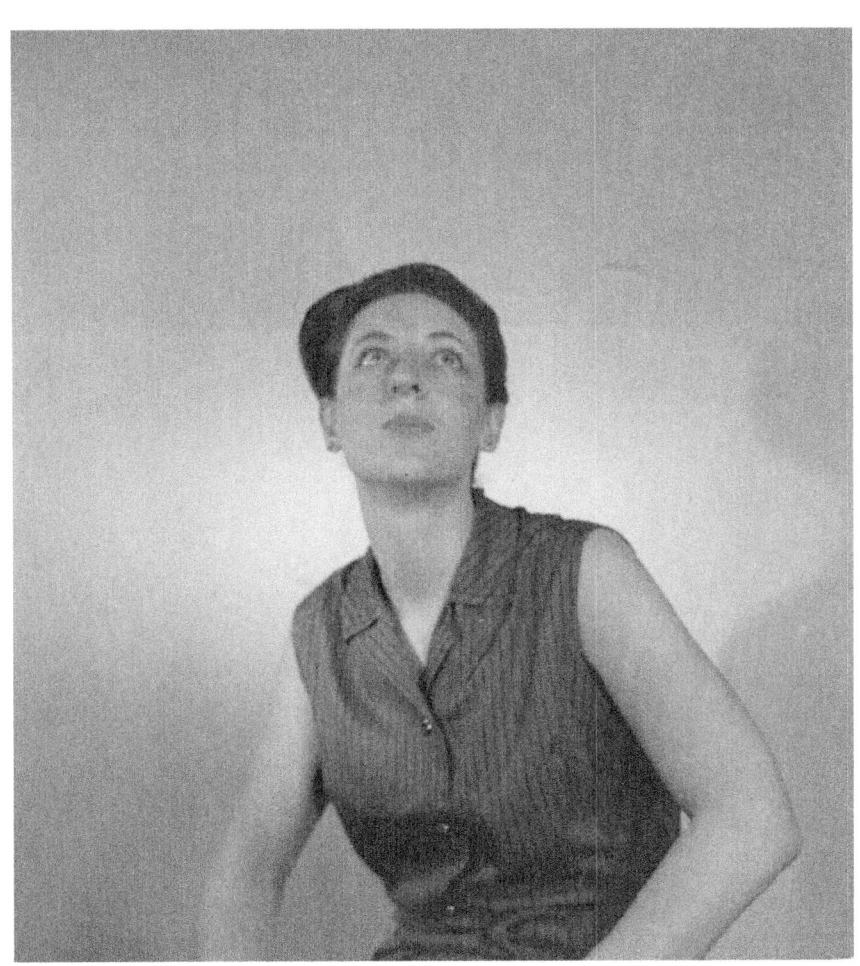

1 EDITOR'S INTRODUCTION

Having had the good fortune to know Jenny for many years, I have come upon the notion of *a Jenny Job* more times than I can count. I can't recall the first time I heard it thrown into the conversational mix, but it's a phrase that has since come into our regular use and reached iconic status. Pulling a fantastic, four-course meal out of a hat, delivered faultlessly, stylishly and with aplomb – *a Jenny Job*. Walking into a boardroom full of men, holding her own and giving as good as she got – *I wasn't going to take that, I did a Jenny Job*. Sailing the high seas, dining at the captain's table, ending up in the epicentre of the ship's social scene every evening – you guessed it.

Jenny has an innate ability to work with any situation she is in, form real connections with people, make them fall hopelessly in love, awe or fascination (and possibly all three) with her – and look a million dollars.

And so to this collection of remembrances, anecdotes and stories, gathered from across a wealth of personal experience, professional pioneering in the electrical industry and sheer *joie de vie*. Jenny asked me to edit this book during the second lockdown at the end of 2020, and it's been my pleasure and privilege, not to mention some much-needed light relief, to have access to her substantial archive of materials, publications, videos, images, notes and achievements – and, of course, her many dinner parties. Incidentally, every single dinner party she has held at home as far back as Christmas Day, 1970 is meticulously catalogued, providing in itself a fascinating history of home entertaining in Britain covering many decades, as well a snapshot of a woman with a great number of close friends who clearly adore her. *A Jenny Job* indeed.

Matt Cresswell
September 2021

2 SATURDAY, 26 AUGUST 1972

It had been an unseasonably cool summer. Bert Foord's TV weather forecast announced a fairly chilly, yet thankfully dry, August Bank Holiday weekend ahead. The summer holidays may have been drawing to a close, but Alice Cooper was still rocking at number 1 in the UK singles chart with *School's Out*. In West Germany, preparations were at full pelt for the summer Olympic Games, which were to kick off that very evening in Munich.

Over in West London, preparations of a very different sort were reaching their climax: Jenny Webb was hosting a dinner party. She and husband, Brian, were about to welcome eight guests to their Richmond home. The kitchen's many electrical appliances were pumping out the heat and light needed to make sure their lovingly-crafted contents would be table-ready at precisely the right time.

Presently, the invited friends arrived, suitably and smartly attired in keeping with the levels of consideration, thought and preparation that had gone in to the planning and execution of one of Jenny's evening occasions. Soon they would be enjoying the very best of electrically-powered home entertaining of the era. Following aperitifs and appetisers, guests were treated to a delicious starter of corned beef pancakes, followed by main course of legendary 1970s staple moussaka, accompanied by cauliflower cheese and carrots. After half an hour or so of after-dinner conversation and the frequent topping up of glasses, knickerbocker glories were presented to the assembled guests, followed by – for those who could still manage them – baby meringues and After Eights. The final element of this gastronomic *tour de force* was cheese and biscuits.

The world was put to rights. Champagne glasses were emptied. Cigarettes were extinguished. Taxis were called. Hugs were warmly given and received. Goodnights were said. And the guests – replete, happy and slightly tiddled – disappeared into the chilly late summer evening.

3 JENNY ARRIVES

Father holding me as a babe in arms, 1939

I was born at 7.20pm on Easter Monday, 10 April 1939 in our home in Lambeth, South London. Both my father and my uncle Tom (my mother's brother) were at the house. In anticipation of my imminent arrival, cake had been provided for the intended visitors, but finding themselves rather peckish whilst awaiting my birth, they decided to eat it. My mother (also named Jenny) was 28 when I was born, and she gave birth without incident, though with the help of the district nurse who kept popping in and out. The first six months of my life were spent in that home in Lambeth.

I didn't meet my father properly until I was six. He had been away fighting in the war and so he was not a part of my very early life as I remember it. My earliest encounter is vague, but I do recall being told to "kiss daddy" and promptly deciding to bite his lip, which had scratchy hairs above it. The only other encounter I can recall with my father in those very early years was in a house that my mother rented in Watford. It had a garden, which I found incredibly exciting, and full of wondrous things to explore. Eating the earth was a favourite pastime (as was, so I am told, the joy of discarding my clothes in it). Father was in bed one morning, and I had a present for him. My mother told me to give it to him, so I climbed the stairs to see him. He looked pleased to see me and said: "Come on darling, come to daddy. Have you got a present for me?" I smiled with innocent pleasure as I opened my hands. Out fell a handful of garden worms, onto his bare chest. He leapt out of bed in double-quick time, as my mother stood by the door laughing at the farcical scene. I was more concerned about the welfare of my worms.

My father was a handsome, vain man. He had large, blue twinkling eyes that seemed to be full of mischief (something I think I inherited). When the war wasn't getting in the way, he was a butcher by trade. He sported a moustache and, at the time, resembled General "Monty". He was the only boy out of five siblings, which went some way to explaining his vanity. His sisters were popular and also very attractive, so much so that artists used them for their sketches, often capturing their hands and eyes in particular. Even my father modelled, and I suppose to some extent it brought in some coppers for the family.

He was not easy to control and often shinned down the drainpipe to go out on the town. He was keen and good at football and even had a tryout for Chelsea. Having followed his father into the butchery trade, he eventually made the grade by becoming a master butcher. With his long absences I, along with many other young children of the time, was raised almost exclusively by my mother.

My father, George Emmerson, during his wartime service

My mother, Jenny Emmerson, whilst pregnant with me

Everybody called my father George, whereas my mother was always *Mrs Emmerson*. She had this sort of demeanour about her. A *style*. My mother was a cook by profession. She had been in service – something at that time that was not thought well of and had quite a stigma attached to it. Her recollections of her times (and her various mishaps) in service struck a chord with me from a very young age, stirring my imagination. I could only wonder about the types of homes she had worked in, the people she had worked for, the appliances she had used and the culinary results she had produced.

She was below the age of 18 and without prior experience when she landed her first job as a cook: providing egg sandwiches for tea. The cooker was of its time – a big black range fueled by coal. She boiled the eggs, then, on removing the shells, found that they were soft. She threw them away and started again with the same result, and so yet again she went through the same procedure. All the while she was aware of the time and got hotter and more flustered by the minute. Finally, after much piling on of coal, she had cooked the eggs to perfection. Making up the sandwiches, she covered them and off they went with the tea. The bell rang. "Jenny, will you come upstairs," said the master in a calm voice. She went as commanded. The master thundered: "What have you been up to with these sandwiches?" Perplexed but not willing to explain the difficulties of the kitchen, she had no reply. She was told to look at them. On examination, she noted that each was beautifully prepared, but to her horror, saw that every single one had a black thumbprint right in the centre. She had been so preoccupied with getting them made, that she had forgotten that her fingers were sooty from the coal range.

On another occasion in a different household she was preparing tea. The solid silver service was the norm. Rather than use hot water to warm the teapot, my mother popped it into the oven, as the heat was low enough. However, the family was late, and mother was forgetful. When at last tea was to be served, she opened the oven to find a molten silver mass. Yet again, she had found herself in trouble.

Somewhere on her travels, she was using a dumb waiter to pass food up from the kitchen to the dining room. Fried fish was being served. Sadly, the person at the top of the waiter dropped the dish, and with it the food tumbled back down the shaft to the kitchen. With little time for niceties and no more fish to fry, she scooped it up, rearranged it on a platter and returned it upwards. It was eaten with nobody ever knowing that the fish had flown.

I wouldn't say my mother was strict as such, but she was

certainly *correct*. I had to behave in a certain manner, and I would know when I had crossed a line. If I played up, she would end up chasing me around the flat with a bamboo stick. She never used to touch me with it if course, but the threat was enough to make me fall into line.

My mother was quite heavy-set, and she hated her build. She was forever on a diet. I remember seeing her in tears over her weight on more than one occasion. I subsequently found out that she had had a nervous breakdown when she was younger, but I never found out the cause and didn't like to pry. Fear of another breakdown haunted her later life, though thankfully never materialised. Yet she was, above all else, a kind woman, and very hospitable. Both my parents were fun, sociable people. Friends were always coming to the house for social calls, parties and dinners. We would gather around the piano, which my father could play by ear. We had a busy, sociable life together.

I was brought up well by my parents. I think because my mother had worked in some very grand houses in her time, she had experienced, and learned to appreciate, certain ways of behaving. She instilled that in me from childhood, and for that I shall be forever grateful. Two of my father's sisters were very glamorous ladies, and I learnt from them how to do my own make-up from a young age. I was brought up surrounded by expectations in terms of how to behave, and also how to look. I was brought up to never let myself down. So, in their different ways, both my mother and father had a profound influence on how I approached my life and the expectations I set for myself.

Etiquette is important because it's all about making other people feel comfortable. It is a courtesy towards others. And my guests tell me when they come for dinner that they love the style of what I do. It takes time on my part to make all the preparations, set the table, ensure everything is nicely organised and neat, and that's before all the food and wine is prepared. When I'm entertaining "properly", I will set my table out two days in advance. Guests appreciate it, and they tell me so. I think we all aspire to create something nice, to do and be better. For me, entertaining and is all about caring for other people. I simply want people I care about to enjoy themselves.

Beyond my parents, I don't really know that much about my wider family. My paternal grandmother was Scottish, and evidently she was married twice. I know that she suffered with her chest, and that as a young boy my father had to go and fetch oxygen cylinders for her whenever she was overcome. She and my grandfather ended up moving to Sutton Dwellings in Chelsea, and she died when my father was 21. He felt her death deeply and was devastated when one day he returned home from work to find that his sisters had given up the flat and left him homeless with nothing. Due to the kindness of a neighbour, a Mrs Trigwell, he at least had a bed for a while.

At some point, his father remarried, and for some unknown reason my aunts always referred to her with venom, so much so that even as I think about it, I cannot recall her name. Needless to say, I never knew my grandfather Emmerson. My maternal grandfather Bowes was a master craftsman, repairing Stradivarius violins for a living. Both my grandmother and my mother laid claim that, through my grandfather, we were related to Queen Elizabeth the Queen Mother, and the Bowes family were indeed very well-placed in Bishop Auckland. If this were the case, then there were rather more secrets and dramas in the closet than I would ever be told. My maternal grandfather left his wife and family to seek his fortune in London before my mother left home, but she used to see him when she, too, came to London and after I was born.

4 THE BOMBS FALL

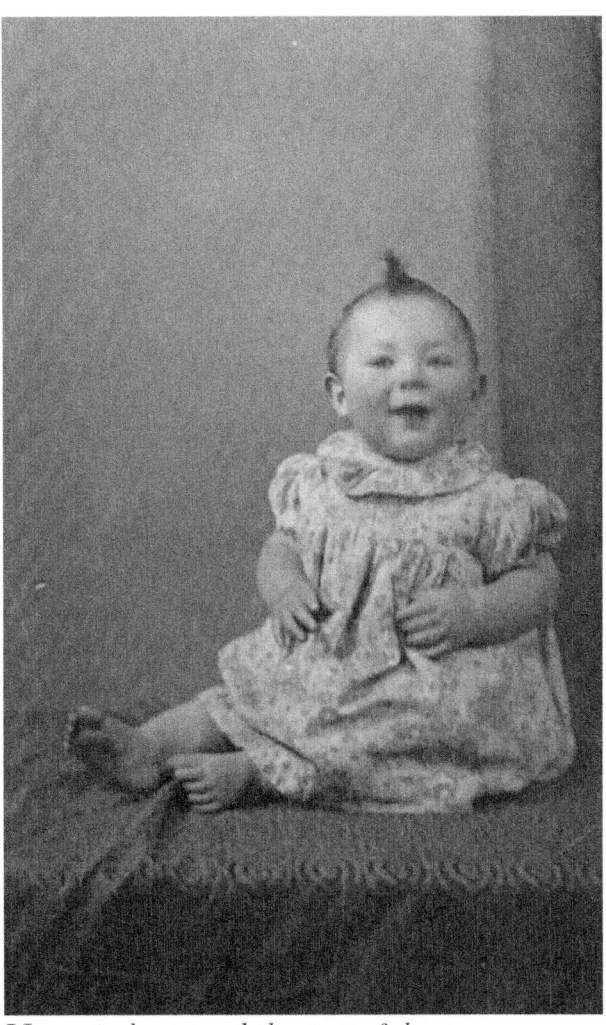

Yours truly, around the start of the war

War was declared in September 1939, when I was five months old. With my father away, my mother raised me alone in a ground-floor flat in Chelsea. My mother's neighbours were the delightfully-named Mrs Bacon and Miss

Mould. We were quite comfortable, having a front room, bedroom, kitchen and toilet. We had gas lighting, and the floors were covered with linoleum. Paintwork was invariably dark brown and the walls were covered with a dark cream gloss, which got darker as the years progressed. Somehow everything always seemed dark. Much later, towards the end of the war, we would move across the road to a top-floor flat in Walton Street, where I would stay until I left to get married in 1960.

Our home was continually cold. The warmest place was directly in front of the fireplace, and although all the rooms had a grate, either the cost of having a fire in each could was too expensive, or there was a shortage of coal. The best place to sit was directly in front of the hearth, and often one side of my legs got so hot that my skin became red-ringed. Meanwhile the offside of the legs remained cold. Anyone taking body space in front of the fire was soon told to move, as they were hogging the heat. In any case, the extremities of a room were not places to spend much time in.

Smoke often billowed into the room when the wind was in the wrong direction, and as a result the smell permeated the remainder of the house. Our windows were ill-fitting and draughts were common. Overall the atmosphere was dark and bleak, with both decorations and furniture taking on the smell and taint of coal dust. This increased throughout the war as more and more buildings were razed to the ground and dust swirled over the immediate area. Much has been made in recent years as to the housewife of years gone by and her fetish for cleaning, but her living conditions left her with little choice.

Making up the fire was an art in itself, and my mother was

the master of it. She terrified the life out of me with her actions, but nevertheless consistently achieved a grand result. Newspaper was twisted into tight strips, and then pieces of wood were laid in a crisscross pattern. On top of this, pieces of coal were placed. She then used a match to ignite the paper and then slowly the wood would start to burn. To speed things up, my mother would take a sheet of newspaper and hold it taut across the fireplace opening. In this way the chimney would act as a funnel and draw the minute flame out. Suddenly there would be a roar as the fire took hold. It was essential to withdraw the newspaper immediately! Every second counted, and if this were not done quickly enough, the paper would catch fire. With total confidence, my fearless mother would squash the burning paper in her hand, and that would be that.

As coal was scarce, lighting the fire was only considered when it was absolutely necessary. Bedroom heating was incredibly rare. Going to bed in the winter was not a pleasant event. Standing on the rug by the bed was better than shivering on the freezing cold lino, but stripping off was terrible as the icy air hit the body. With no form of heating it was not unusual for ice to form on the inside of the windows and giving a frosted effect of various patterns. Speed was of the essence. I would undertake the fast leap into bed, which was of course as cold as the air. Once I'd made the brave leap, it was wiser not to move until my body heat had warmed the sheets.

Sometimes I would use a rubber hot-water bottle to give a bit of localised heat and to cuddle up to once in bed. Rather like making up the fire, filling the bottle was an art. There was no hot water on tap, so mother would fill an aluminium kettle with water and heat it on the gas cooker. Ours had a whistle in a cap which covered the spout. When the water boiled, a piercing screech would continue until the kettle was removed from the heat. Being made of a soft metal, leaks were not uncommon and replacements were not possible, so our kettle also sported round aluminium discs where various repair jobs had been necessary. The bottle stopper was removed and mother would hold the lip away from her body, pouring the hot water in to fill by a half to two-thirds. She would then hold it against her body and gently squeeze it to expel any air. The screw stopper was then inserted. The bottle was a great comforter but there were mornings when either the stopper had not been screwed tightly enough or the rubber had sprung a leak in the night. Then, I would wake up in a bed that was both freezing and soaked in cold water.

Haircare as a child was never a joy, but more like a punishment which, I feel, should be worth recording for the sake of posterity. At the time, very few people had on-tap hot water or an electric kettle, and the most popular cookers were those using gas, where an aluminium kettle or saucepan would be used to heat water. For convenience my mother used a small enamel bowl to hold the water in the kitchen sink, and a china cup to douse my hair. Shampoo was unavailable, conditioner unknown, and electric hairdryers rare. Being young, I had to stand on a chair and bend over the bowl whilst my hair was saturated with cups of water. Then a bar of soap was rubbed and massaged into my hair during which time it was stinging my eyes, and rubbing them with a towel made it worse. Meanwhile, more water was being heated for rinsing, which sometimes was rather more than warm. The next action was to dry the hair as much as possible with a towel. Then a comb was dragged through the wet hair to get rid of the tangles, with the inevitable "ow" as a root was pulled from the scalp. After this, drying continued, but in the winter this would take ages in front of a coal fire, whilst in the summer it would take equally long but in the warmer air. Curls were popular, so, after drying, this next form of torture was being lined up. Curls were achieved by heating curling tongs over a gas flame. The tongs were two slender pieces of metal, and when sufficiently hot, a tress of hair would be wound around one piece of metal, then crushed between the other for a suitable time to ensure a curl. There was an art to the operation. To check that the metal was not too hot, a piece of brown paper was clamped to it. If they were too hot, they would be twirled around in the air by the grips to cool them. Even so, sometimes when they were used too close to the scalp it resulted in a loud yelp from me.

Walton Street was a long thoroughfare, stretching from Draycott Avenue through to Hans Place in Knightsbridge. We lived closer to the Draycott Avenue end, where the houses, except for that of one neighbour, Mrs Nye opposite, opened directly onto the street. Her house had railings, a basement and steps leading up to the front door. It was here that she lived with her son of a similar age to me. Between Mrs Nye's and the Marlborough Buildings was the coal and wood shop called Bulls. The interior was darkened with coal dust and had a permanent smell of coal mixed with that of freshly chopped wood. Upon going inside, to the left there were wooden stalls containing different grades of coal, and to the right a long counter where people ordered their coal and bought bundles of wood for kindling. As the war progressed we would see the mountains of coal diminish. I used to be sent to buy firewood. Behind the counter were stacked neat piles of wood bundles about six inches high tied together with rough string. Each bundle cost 3d.

Coal was delivered by a coalman. The price per bag or hundredweight depended upon the quality selected. Each bag was made of a strong black hessian-type fabric and was about three feet in length. When full they bulged, and coal would almost be tumbling out of the top. Most houses and flats had a special coalhouse or bunker in which to store the coal, often situated within the dwelling. The coal was manually loaded into bags onto a large open-backed lorry, which was forever black from the dust – as was the coalman. Prior to the lorry, I remember the coalman used a two-horse-drawn cart. The coalman usually had a leather cape shoulder covering which would reach over his neck and the back of his head. He would stand with his back to the rear of the lorry and his partner would drag a bag towards the waiting man, who would place one arm up and over his shoulder to grip the top of the bag, and with his other arm support the underside. With a heave he would then move forward for his delivery. In this manner, he would traipse through houses or up endless flights of stairs to make his delivery. On arrival, he tipped himself forward pointing the open top of the bag towards the bunker so that the coal would tumble out into the bunker. Once the weight decreased, the coalman would grip the lower corners of the bag and shake out the remaining dust and coal to make sure that every ounce paid for was given. This would be repeated for several bags regardless of the distance. After delivery, it was clean-up time for the housewife, taking the same route as the coalman had through the house where the coal dust had been trodden in or had inadvertently fallen from the bag. During particularly severe winters, with coal in even shorter supply than usual, families would run into the street to collect any bits of loose coal which had fallen from the bag or lorry during delivery.

Two doors down from Mrs Nye's place was the dairy. This shop was small and pristine with tiled walls and a floor that was kept spotless to the nth degree. It was manned by Mr and Mrs Jones, a Welsh couple who always looked plump and jolly with their pink complexions and white overalls. Mr Jones had a milk cart, upon which there was an enormous brass urn to hold the milk. How it shone and how smart it always looked. Electrical refrigeration was unheard of in ordinary houses, so keeping food fresh was not easy, particularly in the summer. Most people had a larder – either a large built-in cupboard with marble shelves reaching up to the ceiling, or, if space was insufficient, a wall-mounted one with a fine gauze-fronted door to keep the insects out. Muslin covers where draped over food, and for larger items a muslin umbrella was placed over them. Milk and butter were also placed in a container of water, which helped to keep the temperature down. As food was scarce and strictly rationed, storage space was not too difficult, but it was essential to manage it properly. Later, we had huge silver tins of dried deep-yellow egg powder and dried milk - both of which had flavours all their own and not remotely resembling the fresh article.

A few doors further on was the tuck shop. A green-fronted shop owned by a very thin pale lady with long, lank fair hair. I never knew her name and simply called her the *tuck shop lady*. She was wonderful with all us children and we were always allowed to have sweets "on tick" (not for the money as they were paid for, but for the ration coupons). She had a gentle smile, and I am sorry that in my youth I didn't know her or anything about her – beyond being the *tuck shop lady*.

The next main shop was the grocer, Ferguson's, a long, narrow shop with a counter to the left, which was staffed by several men wearing large white aprons. Full of all kinds of wonderful smells, it always seemed that the aroma of fresh coffee wafted through the air of the neighbourhood from here. Fresh sawdust was strewn on the wooden floor, and giant-sized hessian bags of dried goods stood with huge metal scoops atop ready for serving and weighing. Although there were plenty of shops, food was so tightly rationed that we were very limited as to what we could buy.

Memories can dim after many decades, but I believe that the next main shop was the butcher. Turning the corner into Draycott Avenue was the Home and Colonial, another grocery shop and, further along, a bakery, where the reassuring smell of freshly-baked bread was the norm. Opposite, there were stalls of greengroceries. The Lay family manned these and they were well-known to all. Further along was the chemist, and next to him, Holland's the hardware shop, which sold everything required for home maintenance from a single nail to a gas mantle. It had a dark interior, bare wood floors and smelt of paraffin. Here there was also an open-fronted wet fish shop displaying shiny fish on a white-and-black tiled display counter. Mr Miller, the owner, always looked clean and smart with his white overalls and his boater perched in a straight manner on his head. On the corner nearby there was a picture frame shop owned by Mr Januse, a short, dark, portly man who was considered to be a cut above the mere tradesman. Everyone regarded him with some respect.

On our side of Walton Street, towards Draycott Avenue, there were two shops I remember well. Mrs Long's paper shop, the newsagents where we would get our daily paper along with the occasional magazine such as *Picture Post*. Closer to us was the Sunlight Laundry, where we could take clothes to be washed and then collected, or for those with more money, to be ironed as well. The shop was locally known as the bag wash. A plump peroxide blonde served here, enveloped in a white wraparound overall. Those using the service were provided with a table listing garments and household linen. Each person had an identification number written onto a tape, which was sewn to each article. The housewife would tick off the list and give the quantity of the laundry to be washed. It would then be placed in one or more of the pillowcases and taken to the shop. A van would arrive once or twice daily to collect the dirty laundry and deliver the washed. When collected, the housewife would then check the items against her original list.

Living in London, laundry was often done in this way but was only one of several choices. Often, the local council had wash houses. In the flats where we lived later, there were wash houses installed on the roof of each block. An enclosed building with windows, it had a bank of deep wooden sinks, a stone copper and an enormous metal mangle which accommodated two wooden roller pins which, as the laundry was fed into them, were turned at the same time by a handle fixed to a large wheel. It was no easy operation trying to get the wet laundry fed into the rollers whilst turning the great wheel! Many homes had a scullery where they had their own washing equipment, and the method used was still based on what had been going on at the beginning of the twentieth century.

At the top of Walton Street was Harrods and this was a place that we all took for granted. They claimed that they could get anything in the world, even an elephant! Somehow, I think that this claim did not apply during the war years. Harrods was a local shop for me, so it was not unusual to spend time there. The central area of the ground floor was very impressive, being made of marble and with seating along the centre. Here also was a banking area and people would sit watching the world go by. I somehow remember nannies with prams, but perhaps that is just my imagination. They also had a pets department on one of the upper floors, and it was here that my mother always took visiting children. Different animals and birds were a part of the department, so for children it was quite a thrill. On one occasion, my mother said to us, would we like to hold one of the caged mice. The answer was obvious so she told us to look out for any staff and then carefully put her hand into the cage to get a mouse. As she removed it, it jumped from her hand and scuttled away. We children thought it was funny, but were a little frightened as to what would happen. Being my mother, she ignored the whole event and quickly ushered us from the department. I wonder if its descendants are still there to this day?

Throughout the war, we seemed to live in perpetual darkness. Street lighting was not allowed, added to which it was often non-existent due to the bombing which took out the gas and electricity supplies. Every house had to have a blackout at every window. Ours were large black curtains. Should any house show the smallest glimmer of light then a warden would soon be banging on the door.

Dust was very common due to the destruction of so many buildings and bombed sites were often the playgrounds for London children. We loved them with all the rubble upon which to clamber, and of course the many hiding places. Some houses still had partial rooms standing within the chaos, even staircases and cupboards could be intact, and for any youngster it was all a massive adventure. Mothers must have been beside themselves with worry about their offspring's adventures, but we were in heaven. We were told not to play on such sites and not to pick anything up, but of course we did. One day I arrived home with a stuffed parrot still intact in its glass case. What tears I had when told to throw it away. The reason, it was crawling with bugs. Bugs were yet another problem and with the destruction of the houses any small creature from the depths of a building would be unearthed.

Smog was another part of life, and even before the great smog of 1952, during daylight hours it would envelope everything. Always damp and dark, it could be seen swirling as it passed any light. It seemed to change the most familiar of places and silently obscured everything within a few feet. Every step was, as a child, one of fear as the path unfolded before me. It also made everything echo, so the tapping of a stick, the clip-clopping of a horse, the sound of a car or even the steps of a walker magnified. I would become really frightened. The bombs did not cause me any great distress, but the smog was my living nightmare. Getting lost in the fog was not unusual especially at nighttime, particularly with familiar local landmarks being razed.

Not all homes had a bathroom, thus we would often have a weekly bath in a long galvanised bathtub which everyone took turns to sit in. Usually placed in front of the fireplace, it was enclosed by a wooden clotheshorse over which towels were draped to give a small amount of privacy. An arduous job, the water was heated in buckets on the hob of the cooker and then poured into the bath. As the water cooled, a kettle was kept on the boil to top up at the appropriate time. After this, it was emptied using a bucket and then when the bath was lighter and easier to move, it was lifted and the remaining water poured down the sink.

Chelsea had its own bathhouse and I did experience it on a number of occasions. Within the building there was a huge white tiled room with separate bathrooms partitioned off. Each was self-enclosed and accommodated a huge white vitreous enamel bath with great chunky brass water taps. By the side of the bath sat a wooden slatted stool, a slatted bath board and a large hook behind the door. The attendant sat outside and was responsible for the cleaning of the bath and supplying water as required. She could also supply warm, soft fluffy bath towels for which extra was charged in addition to the sixpence already paid, but many took their own towels. It was a wonderful, warm slightly steamy atmosphere. In this blissful world all you would hear was people calling: "More hot water please in number two" or whatever the number of their bathroom was. Bathing was never mixed so there were separate sessions for women and for men, and a set time was given for each bather.

Having being born at the outset of the war, I grew up in a world where danger was, to me, an everyday occurrence. Living with the daily threat of bombardment was just normal for me, and for everyone I knew. Bomb shelters were constructed in back gardens, some were underground but many, like ours, were simply a building in the back yard. Upon hearing the sirens, here we would huddle, wrapped in blankets and eiderdowns, with a flask of tea and perhaps a sandwich. Nobody knew how long an air raid would last. Another basic need was a bucket, which served as a toilet. During a raid it was unsafe to leave the shelter, so the needs of nature had to be met somehow. Toilet paper was not readily available, so we would cut newspapers into squares, pierce the corners with a hole and thread string through so the resulting item could be hung by the side of the toilet pan.

Many people took to the Underground stations, and at a specified time they would all traipse on to the platforms with their various belongings to spend sometimes the whole night underground. I well remember getting off the Tube and, with my mother, picking our way through the crowds of people. As a child it seemed to be a jolly place with lots of chatter and music from mouth organs. I was rather sad not to be a part of such a happy throng. Of course, I was unaware of the implications. I can recall adults talking about a direct hit on the Tube, where huge doors were battened down to stop the entire network from being flooded, but in the process, everyone within that area was trapped and drowned. It was said that they would remain there forever. I don't know whether this actually happened, but such a tragedy would be awful if true.

Everyone had to carry a gasmask, and as children had to be encouraged to use theirs, ours were made of red rubber rather than the black the adults had, and with a flapping thin nose. It was commonly known as the Mickey Mouse gasmask. These were great fun, as if you blew out it could be made to shudder and vibrate. However, the smell of the mask was most unpleasant, and I hated it. Many years later I donated mine to the Museum of Richmond.

Throughout the war, rumours circulated as to the best place to take shelter and survive if a bomb fell on the house. This was based on the observations made looking at those houses which had been bombed. Two of the popular choices were built-in cupboards or under the staircase. We had both in Walton Street. I can remember hearing the sirens warning of an imminent attack, the sound of bombs dropping, the building shaking and the guns (they were locally known as Big Berthas) shooting into the skies at Hyde Park. None of these held any fear for me: it was what I was brought up with. My mother would say: "There's daddy, chasing away the Germans." For whatever reason, there was a time when my mother followed the local chatter and I recall at the sound of the siren she would wrap me in an eiderdown, cradle me in her arms and then stand in the full length built-in cupboard having closed us inside. She stood like this with me in her arms until the raid was over. For a time, we also used the space under the staircase, but I think that this must have been when I became too heavy to hold. Eventually we had a shelter built in the yard at the rear of the house, and I was well drilled in my actions. As soon as I heard the sirens, my little fat legs would run as fast as possible to the shelter whilst clutching my feather eiderdown (this was considered to give extra protection in the case of a direct hit). Here the adults would sit talking, knitting and singing.

With the Doodlebugs, we would hear them coming with a constant loud rattling sound, then all activities would cease: there was a silence for a few moments before it plummeted to the ground, followed by a tremendous explosion. A common remark at the time was: "I wonder who caught that one." The pattern of noise was always the same. The siren would sound, and far away towards the south coast one could hear the guns firing. Initially it was a faint *boom boom boom*, and then the planes and bombs reached London and the noise of the Hyde Park guns could be clearly heard. The shooting and noise were phenomenal with guns, planes and bombs exploding and the sound of fire engine bells ringing into the night.

Another story, which I can vaguely remember as a family

story, was often repeated around that time. My parents' bed was placed under an enormous window. On reflection, it was the only place in the room where it could be accommodated. My father was home on leave and in bed when the sirens sounded. My mother tried to persuade him to move to the shelter in the yard, but he would have none of it. Thus, my mother and I departed. The raid was fierce, heavier than usual. Suddenly there was an enormous explosion, the shelter shook and trembled, and visibility was down to nil. For a moment there was silence, and then we heard my father: "Help, I've been buried, we've been hit." Holding my mother's hand we rushed to the house, which had no windows left but appeared to be without other damage. The tone of my father's voice indicated he had not been injured. My mother cautiously opened the bedroom door – and started to giggle, and then to laugh. Creeping from behind her, I saw a body frantically fighting under the bedclothes. It was my father. He had been enveloped in the falling window blackout curtains, which had been dislodged by the vibration. My mother thought it very funny, especially as she lived with bombing raids on a daily basis. My father was not amused, got up and said that he was going back to his barracks, as it was safer there!

One day, quite early on in the war, my father arrived home with a gift: a Pekinese dog. It was a delightful creature and very friendly. My mother, knowing my father, remarked that it was obviously a pedigree and asked how he had come upon it. He said that he had met a Canadian soldier in a pub in Watford, who, as he was being sent overseas, wanted his pet to go to a good home. Father had given him a few pounds and returned to Chelsea with his present. Having completed his leave, he then returned to his camp. Walton Street, where we lived, led into Draycott Avenue, and the next road was Sloane Avenue. In all, that was about a five- or ten-minute walk. Our little dog was fine and went out daily with my mother and me to the local shops. Some months passed, then one October day there was a knock at the door. Two policemen were standing there with a lady. The police asked my mother whether she had a dog. She replied that she did, and had done so for nearly a year. She explained how it had come into our possession. The police officer then said that they had reason to believe that it was a valuable dog stolen from a block of private flats, The Cloisters, in Sloane Avenue, and the lady with them was the owner. My mother brought the dog to the door, and as soon as it saw the lady it went mad with excitement. The police confirmed that they would not prosecute, but that was the last we saw of our pet, the policeman having given my mother a receipt (of all things) for the dog. A small world: the Canadian had been based in Chelsea, had stolen the dog and gone with it to Hertfordshire, where my father bought it, only to return it to the very place from which it had been taken.

As my mother's family was from the north, we would sometimes visit them. To me, the world was full of people in uniforms of every colour and style. I would frequently see men with badly-scarred, misshapen faces, but I had no fear of them, as there were so many. At the time I was told that they had been burned fighting Hitler and there was nothing to consider unusual. Later we saw our first Americans and I remember thinking how strange that they were always so smart and handsome. They, too, seemed very kind and it was not unusual for children to trot up to them, saying: "Have you any gum, chum?" It seemed that I was missing out, so one day I asked the question. I was given gum but my mother was furious when I told her how it had been obtained. The threats left me in no doubt as to what would happen if I ever did it again. Thus, I was one of the few children in the neighbourhood who did not enjoy a supply of that wonderful substance with which one could compete to blow bubbles.

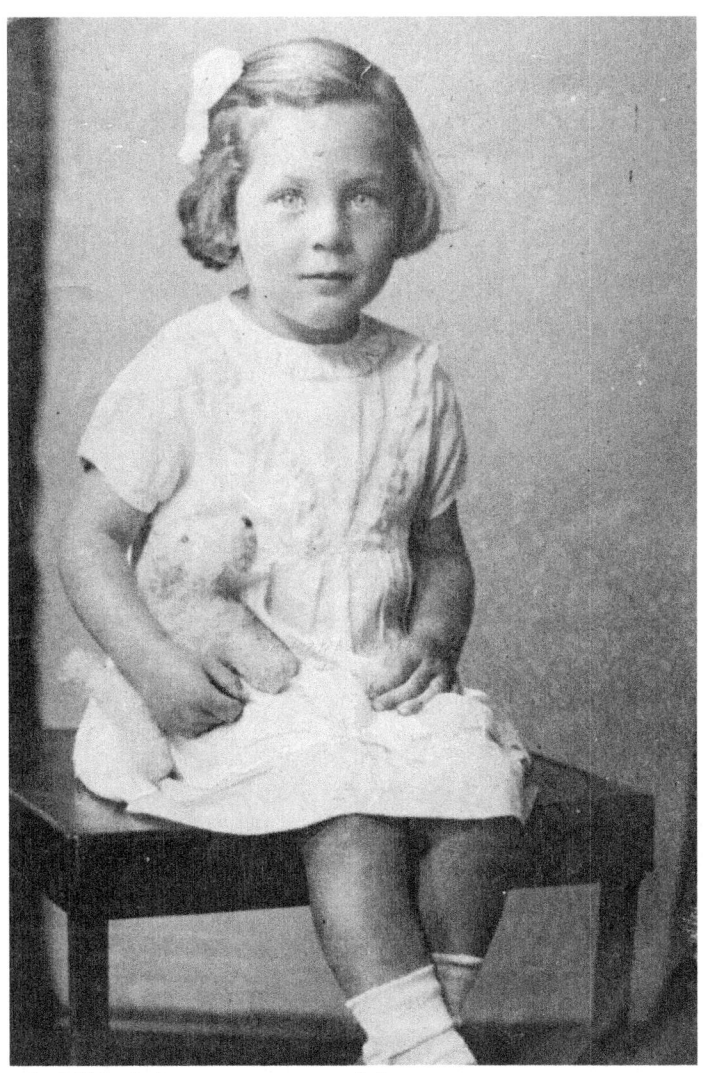

A child of the war – me aged four

The mainline stations were always noisy, smelling of coal and steamy from the coal-fired trains. Most men, and many women, were in uniform carrying big sausage-shaped bags slung over their backs, and everyone had a box within which was their gasmask. The trains were full to bursting, and to move along a corridor was a major hike as people squeezed through the kit bags, luggage and bodies. It was the same in the individual compartments, although some luggage could be put onto the luggage rack. As my mother was travelling with a young child, everyone would try to be helpful and I would be lifted across the heads of people and placed in the luggage rack where I could sleep and also give my mother a chance of a little comfort without me on her lap. Because of the war and the threat of attack, the lighting was very low and I think blue, and all the blinds on the train were pulled down. The trains always seemed to move very slowly and the journeys to be endless. I now wonder if the slowness was to avoid the emission of steam which could have alerted any enemy aircraft circling above.

As a young child at the end of the war I would travel alone. My mother would ask the guard to keep an eye on me and to put me off at the right station where my grandmother would meet me. Each compartment accommodated about eight people, and there was always a *Ladies Only* compartment near to the guard's van, thus I would be on my way, usually with a packet of jam sandwiches. The travellers were always very kind and generous, thus I was well-fed and cared for throughout the journey.

During and shortly after the war, my mother and I took occasional holidays to her friends in Hexham, Northumberland. One day, one of the friends, Mrs Cesford, was speaking with a woman at her front door. After a short while, she called to me and asked if I had taken some apples from a tree in her neighbour's garden. Having replied yes, she explained that this was not allowed without permission, and as I had not eaten them she asked me to return them. However, being a city child, apples were very rare for me and I assumed that each would have a different taste. Thus, on returning them, and to the horror of both women, I had taken a bite out of every apple! On another visit, Mrs Cesford went into her garden to find that only the tulip stalks were visible and all the flower heads had gone. Oh dear, once again my curiosity had got me into trouble!

Travelling for me was no problem, and in London, apart from the buses and the Tube, I was well able to hail a cab from a very young age. I am not sure if there is a method which should be used but simply standing at the kerb and raising one's hand high into the air always seemed to bring results (and still does). Flapping hands and an agitated appearance were not the way to do it. Travel, for business and for pleasure, would become a major part of my life later on, and I wonder if this is due to my early experiences on the railway.

One of my weekly treats was to visit the Chelsea Palace variety theatre at the top of Sidney Street off the King's Road. We always sat in the cheapest seats – "the gods" – in the upper circle. During the interval, a spotlight was used to move around the audience in the stalls and circle tiers, and eventually would stop on a member of the audience. On this particular evening, it stopped and highlighted me. The prize awarded was a food parcel wrapped in one of the very large posters which had advertised the previous week's show. However, to get it, it had to be presented on the stage. Thus, I was escorted all the way down the stairs, along a corridor and finally onto the stage but then as the parcel was so heavy so I had to return the same way with an usher carrying it for me! I was thrilled to have such a prize and indeed, it was the first occasion, but by no means the last, that I ever stood on a theatre stage. As a child, I always wanted to be an actress. I wanted to be famous. Actually I think that what I ended up doing later on in life was far more difficult than being an actress. If you're an actress, you have a persona to hide behind. Doing what I did, I had to stand up and promote and sell myself.

Although I have vivid memories of the war itself, I can't remember the *end* of it. I know that I was very much there, however, as there is photographic evidence, of sorts. One of the children assembled at a long trestle table at a street party in Chelsea in the wake of VE Day is me, although my face is unfortunately hidden from view. All that can be seen is my little paper hat poking up. So I know I was there, but I just can't see myself, nor remember it!

VE Day celebrations: my hat can be seen, fourth along on the right!

5 A LONDON CHILDHOOD

With my father in the West End, 1949

The local school was within walking distance from my home and accommodated both primary and junior children. It was the same one that my father had attended and several of the teachers were still teaching in my time. Called The Marlborough School, it was an old Victorian building covering several floors. The playground area was in the front, and there were separate entrances for boys and girls. Indeed, over each - and set in the stone - it clearly read: Boys - Girls. The classes were mixed. One classroom in particular had deep tiered steps on which wooden desks with flip-down seats were situated. Each had an inkwell fitted into the top, and we used a thin piece of wood, at the end of which was a nib. To write, we would dip the nib into the inkwell. This was an art in itself. Too much ink would result in a big blob on the paper, too little and it would not be sufficient to write with. A continuous action of frequent dipping and writing was the norm. Another problem was should one put too much pressure on the nib. It would bend the point or even break it.

At the front, the teacher would sit, near a portable blackboard which was the main teaching aid. There was always a smell of chalk dust as the white stick of chalk powdered as it was etched against the board. As the teacher wrote, one could hear the tap of the chalk as he or she applied it for the next word. At times there would be a squeak as the chalk did not make the right contact. Chalk was also used by many teachers as a missile! Should a child be giving less than total attention, it would be hurled without warning at the offender and usually hit its mark.

The format of each day was always the same. A huge handheld bell was rung by a teacher in the playground, whereupon we would get into line and then quietly troop into the hall. Here, we had assembly which included prayers and hymns. We always sang *New Every Morning* and *Jerusalem*.

Once over, we dispersed to our various classrooms which led off from the hall itself. No chatting in the room was allowed, and as soon as an adult came in we had to stand and in unison say "Good morning". Adults were always addressed by their title and surname. At mid-morning, we had a break from lessons and were given small bottles of milk to drink. A child would be selected to be milk monitor and it was for them to pass it to other children from crates and put the empty bottles back.

My first form mistress was a horror. Thus, a story. Her name Miss Geary, and she had also taught my father. She was a short heavy woman, and had a figure of a plump woodpigeon. Her short blonde hair was in fact of a light gold colour with set waves throughout. She wore heavy make-up and always bright-red lipstick. She had excellent posture and tended to strut as she walked. We were absolutely terrified of her. She smoked De Maurier cigarettes and often would send one of us to the local shop to buy a box should she run out of them.

During lessons, she would summon a child to her desk with regard to their work. Then, if she was displeased, she would suddenly lash out, sending the poor child spinning backwards. This never happened to me, but I used to dream that if it did, she would hit me so hard that I would fall out of the first-floor open window and then she would get into trouble. No child ever told their parents, as we were even more fearful of possible revenge. However, I had a tendency to talk in my sleep and evidently one night I woke up crying. It took some time, but eventually my mother got the story from me. She went to the school – much to my distress – and reported Miss Geary. I was moved to another class with a new teacher, Mr Bailey. From then on, I was able to learn.

Outside of school, the weekends were naturally a highlight of my young life. Saturdays were huge fun. In the mornings I, along with hundreds of other children, would go to the Saturday morning pictures. Our local Gaumont cinema was almost opposite Chelsea Town Hall. Full of excitement we would sit waiting for the Cowboys-and-Indians film to start, having paid our sixpenny entrance fee. Before this, we would have our song on the screen and we all sang (or some would say shouted) the words:

We come along on Saturday morning greeting everybody with a smile.
We come along on Saturday morning knowing it's all worthwhile.
As members of the junior club we all intend to be.
Good citizens as we grow up, and champions of the free.
We come along on Saturday morning greeting everybody with a smile.
Smile, smile, greeting everybody with a smile.

Children had a simple life. Routine was a major part of it, and under-fives were always put to bed to sleep for an hour every afternoon. Older children, when not at school, could go out to play. Good manners were essential, and to question any adult was a cardinal sin. *Children should be seen and not heard* was the motto of most households. We would have to sit still and listen whilst the adults talked, and woe be tied any child who was brave enough to move. If a slap on the legs was not possible at the time I knew that on our return home I would be suitably chastised and sent to bed. Such behaviour was also expected in public places. I well remember being in the china department of Peter Jones department store in Sloane Square. I moved from my given spot. Without hesitation, I was marched from the shop, smacked hard on the legs, whisked home and sent to my room for the rest of the day. Such lessons were not uncommon, as I never seemed to learn.

During, and just after, the war, children had few toys as these were not being manufactured and money was short. Our main gifts were at Christmas and birthdays. I was lucky and had Enid Blyton books, a doll, a teddy bear and later a dolls' house, pram and portable radio. These were the main presents of my childhood. When I got older, my godfather, uncle Tom (who had eaten the cake when I was born) would always give me two pairs of Aristoc stockings.

I never felt deprived. I would spend time with other children, playing Cowboys-and-Indians, Nurses and *The Daring Dexters*. This was based on the regular radio programme about a circus family. Depending on their age, most children belonged to the Sunday school, Cubs, Brownies, Guides, Scouts or the local youth club. I loved dancing, as did most of my friends, and I used to go to ballet and tap-dancing classes. The teacher was a Miss Duval, and she held her classes in the basement of a house in Sidney Street, Chelsea, just off the King's Road. We had to wear a short, straight sleeveless black tunic with a slit on either side. Most had to be made at home and mine was made from black satin which had been used as blackout material. Miss Duval was also an artist and over the years painted my portrait on more than one occasion. My parents bought one and I have it to this day. In 2008, I became curious about Miss Duval and so I wrote to the Royal Academy for any information relating to her. They replied, and I was surprised to learn that her full name was Dorothy Zinaida Duva, born in 1917. She died in 1970, and she had exhibited her work at the Academy from 1940-1961. Interestingly for me, her 1945 work, a still life painting, was entitled *98 Sydney Street, SW3*, and it was indeed here that she had both her dance studio in the basement, and her artist studio on an upper floor.

From the information I received, she was regarded as a talented artist, having studied at the Slade School of Fine Art from 1949 to 1955, is listed in The Dictionary of British Artists 1900-1950, was a Fellow of the British Academy, was awarded a silver medal at the Paris Salon in 1960 and later the Academy Italia gold medal, and interestingly, the Grenadier Guards commissioned her to paint the portrait of Victoria Cross winner Harry Nicholls. Her CV has so much more to tell, so her painting of me is even more special. The Royal Academy confirmed however that no painting of me was ever hung in any of the exhibitions of her work there.

Portrait of me painted by Miss Duval

As there were about ten children living in our flats, most had birthday parties in each other's homes, and all had a similar format. Several mothers looked after us and organised the events. We girls would be in our best dresses with ribbons in our hair, and the boys in their best trousers and shirts and sometimes even a jacket. We would give a small birthday gift which was usually wrapped in brown paper and secured with string. The dining table would be covered with a table cloth and laden with the party fare, all of which was always homemade and seemed to be the same at every party. It was mainly flavoured jelly, blancmange, jam and savoury paste sandwiches, small jam tarts, butterfly cakes, and the birthday cake. I remember that no child ever had an allergy nor refused the food offered, but always ate everything with gusto. The homemade butterfly cakes were small fairy cakes with the tops sliced off which were then cut in half to represent the wings of a butterfly and held in a "V" position on the top of the cake with butter icing. The birthday cake too was a homemade Victoria sandwich with either butter cream, jam or both, and topped with white or coloured icing, into which small candles fitted with holders were pushed.

We would be seated around the table for the tea party, which concluded with singing *Happy Birthday*, whilst the lit candles on the birthday cake were blown out and a small slice of cake served. Depending on the household we would say grace prior to eating. Everyone was well-behaved and would wait for the adult present to offer the food. There was no helping oneself. After tea, the adults would organise games, which generally included Pass the Parcel, Blind Man's Buff, Pin the Tail on the Donkey, the Tray Game, the Aeroplane Game, and any party pieces. My performance piece was always the song *You Are My Sunshine* and my cousin Georgie's, a recitation. He never wanted to perform, so he gave it at high speed – and was unable to sound his aitches. Thus, it went:

'Arry went to 'Ampstead
'Arry lost 'is 'at
'Arry's mother said to 'im
Where is your 'at?
'Anging on the 'anger in the 'all.

I think that the Tray Game was designed to calm us down after an excitable time. We were given a pencil and paper and then a covered tray was brought in. Once the cover was removed, we were given a short time to memorise the various items placed on it, and then the tray was taken away. The point of the game was to write down all the items you could remember, and the child who got the most received a modest prize.

The Aeroplane Game was really special and unique and was only ever experienced at Georgie's home. Waiting outside the room for our turn we would hear the squeals of the child who had just been blindfolded and taken into the "airport". When my turn came, I was guided to the "plane" to stand in a certain place, and I was told to hold the shoulder of one of the mothers on either side of me. I was then "flying" and felt the sensation of going up and down whilst at the same time one of the mothers would explain where I was, as I was totally disorientated and needed to be told how high I was going. Finally, I was told to jump! I believed that I was really high when in fact I was only inches from the floor – it was merely in my mind – and my flying had been achieved by standing on a small plank of wood held by the mothers who raised and lowered it in small degrees from the floor. After the first time, everyone at Georgie's parties knew what would happen, but the thrill was always there.

Parties were always enjoyable, and as we said thank you for a lovely time and goodbye, we were given a piece of birthday cake wrapped in a paper napkin to take home. Simple memories are sometimes the best.

In the afternoons at the weekend, my mother would take me to lunch at the Strand or Marble Arch Lyons' Corner House, then onto the cinema or a matinée theatre performance. The Strand Corner House was situated next to Charing Cross railway station. Here we would be seated on plush red velvet seats and a pianist would be gently playing. My mother would ask for a newspaper and it would be brought to her with a long stick threaded through it so the pages would not sag as she turned them. In the early days, a high chair was brought for me thus I was able to survey all. The waitresses were always chirpy and cheerful but very correct in their manner and their dress. They wore black dresses with long sleeves, white frilly caps and aprons, dark stockings and black shoes. Tights at that time had not been introduced, so it had to be stockings! My personal choice of menu varied little: breaded plaice and chips with a bread roll and butter followed by a knickerbocker glory, which at 2/6 was expensive.

A cinema trip to the West End was always special. Not only did we see the film, but during the interval an organ would rise from the bowels of the auditorium in the pit in front of the screen like a musical monster, and a musician dressed in a black suit, white shirt and black dickie-bow would play the latest tunes. Often my mother would order tea prior to the interval. This was brought to our seats and served on a doily-covered tray with a china teapot, hot water jug, milk jug, cups and saucers and a plate of biscuits. Saturday was certainly a day apart. As TV was not common until 1953, the evening would usually be spent at home listening to the radio. Popular programmes of the day included *The Daring Dexters*, *Dick Barton Special Agent*, the *Tommy Hanley Show* and an evening play.

Sunday was usually the same. It started with my parents reading the newspapers in bed, then the wonderful smell of mother cooking our breakfast of fried eggs, bacon, bread and tomatoes. I can still smell it now. After breakfast, I had extra chores to do to earn my pocket money. A great sum of a shilling which, I thought, was not enough. My chores included dusting, taking and collecting the bag wash and, on a Sunday, cleaning the silver, not that we had much to clean. I hated it: it was fiddly and dirty on the hands. Years later, my mother told me that she hated housework so was rather pleased to use me. Once finished, I could go out to play before lunch. For a time, my father used to try to take me for a walk. I say "try", as no sooner were we outside than it became a battle of wills. Should he wish to go left I would want to go right, and indeed vice versa. The inevitable consequence was getting my legs soundly slapped and sent home. The walk never lasted, but possibly suited my father. To explain, a friend's mother stopped my mother one day to say that she was most embarrassed as she and her husband were not church people. My mother was puzzled for a while and then roared with laughter. I had been told that my father was going to church before Sunday lunch, thus, I repeated this to my friend, Valerie. In fact, he was going to the local pub, The Enterprise, for a drink.

My mother was an excellent cook and Sunday lunch was always good. The aroma of roasting meat, boiling vegetables and cooked pastry was tantalising. Always served after the pub closed at 3pm, we would sit and enjoy the roast of the day with all the trimmings. Beef with Yorkshire puddings, lamb with mint sauce and pork with apple sauce, always served with roast potatoes and other vegetables, and invariably followed with some delicious pudding and custard. Once over, I would make my way to St Simon's Church for Sunday school. Many children were walking to the same place and nobody poked fun, as it was an accepted way of life. When a little older, I became a Sunday school teacher and taught the younger ones with stories from the Bible. On special church festivals, all the children would attend the service. Two of these, I especially remember. On Mothering Sunday we would be given a posy of violets and during the service we would present them to our respective mothers. The other was the Harvest Festival. Being in London, we had to buy produce to take to the church. I used to get a free small wicker basket from the greengrocer which I filled with crumpled paper on top of which I artistically (or so I thought) arranged an orange, apple, carrot, potato and any other fruit or vegetable which we could afford. The church was wonderfully decorated, and the smell of the fruit, vegetables, bread and flowers was very distinctive. My two favourite hymns were always sung, and I joined in with gusto: *We Plough the Fields and Scatter* and *Now the Harvest's Gathered In*.

After church there was little to do except go for a walk in Hyde Park or visit the museums in Exhibition Road. The latter were very popular. Our favourite was the Natural History Museum (we called it the "Animal Museum") and the Science Museum. We would dash around finding old and new favourites, but the whale and the dinosaur would always be the best. Then onto the children's area in the basement of the Science Museum. Here we would swirl knobs and press buttons to get action from the small figures behind a glass panel to plough the field or turn the well handle. Then onto the "magic door" which would automatically close and open as we walked through a beam of light. Much later, in the 1980s, I took a young boy to see this with other exhibits, and he was not impressed. By this time automatic doors were a part of life. On reflection, we children saw a great deal and understood little but it was a simple way to educate us. All too early, the museums would close and the guardians would usher us out.

Sunday tea was yet another special event. In the winter, we would toast bread and currant buns in front of the fire. A long, three-pronged fork was used to pierce the bread or bun and then held in front of the flames until browned, whereupon the procedure was repeated on the other side. The taste was special due to the smoke from the fire and the unevenness of browning. Sometimes there would be a mishap when the bread fell off the fork into the fire and then retrieval was urgent before it went up in flames. Salad was another Sunday food. Crisp lettuce, firm flavoursome tomatoes, sliced cucumber and hard-boiled eggs plus delicious delicacies such as shrimps, prawns, cockles or winkles and a plate of bread and butter. Earlier in the day, a man would come round the streets with a long, low wooden barrow laden with shellfish. I would offer to get our fish and would run off with a white china basin into which, using a metal ladle or mug, he would measure the shellfish into my receptacle. What a joy it was to peel the shrimps or prawns and then suck at the slightly sweet flesh, or remove the black round covering to the winkle and, with a pin, pull out with art the complete winkle. This was our only food shopping experience on a Sunday.

I cannot remember the reason why, but in 1948, at the grand

age of nine, I decided to leave home. I do remember that I had some sort of tiff with my mother and I was going to teach her a lesson. At the time of my altercation, a friend of hers was visiting and to emphasise my point I went to my bedroom, packed some clothes into a small suitcase and put on my coat. Being ready to leave I returned to the sitting room and asked for my ration book which she gave me without any discussion. I then flounced into the hall and made sure that I shut the front door with an almighty bang. Having not left the flat, I crept back into my bedroom and with my case, hid in the wardrobe waiting for her reaction. I waited and waited whilst she continued talking to her friend without even mentioning my departure. After what seemed an age, I finally revealed myself and without a word of my escapade my mother simply treated me as if nothing had happened. Now, on reflection, all I can say is what a wise woman she was.

Every year after the war, the Sunday school had an outing for all the children. A coach would take us to the seaside. Our mothers would prepare a packed lunch and most of us would board carrying it in a brown paper parcel tied with string. Plastic carrier bags and sellotape were non-existent. Many foods were still on ration or not available, thus the contents were usually jam or paste sandwiches. As sliced bread was not available, the depth of the sandwiches was dependent upon how well a mother could slice the bread. By the time we reached our destination, they always seemed to be squashed, misshapen and a bit soggy. Even so, we ate them with gusto. Then it was time to enjoy the beach or gardens by playing games and taking a dip in water, which was always icy. Late afternoon would herald our return and we would clamber onto the coach, often singing songs such as *Old McDonald Had a Farm, One Finger One Thumb Keep*

Moving and *Ten Green Bottles* - but soon there would be peace as everyone had exhausted themselves.

One year we went to Little California and visited a park with a lake. It's worth highlighting that clothes and shoes were not in abundance in those days. I was rather pleased with the sandals I was wearing: they were new but belonged to my mother as we took the same shoe size. I was only about ten years old, and felt very grown up. We had our picnic and I was sitting with a group of children. Everyone was busy enjoying themselves and playing games. Other groups of children from elsewhere were a part of the scene, most of whom had been brought from London for the day.

By the edge of the lake a small low wall had been erected, and everyone had been warned to keep away from the water as it was deep. I saw a small child who seemed too close. He then climbed onto the wall and started waddling along it. Suddenly, the child overbalanced and toppled off the wall into the lake. He was splashing and sinking and moving further out at the same time. The child was drowning and nobody was aware of it. I ran to the wall, jumped in and made my way to the boy, grabbed him and started to pull him out of the water. It all happened in moments. Adults were at the side hauling us out and clustering around the crying little one. I left to rejoin our group where dry clothes were being heaped onto me. I felt so embarrassed, especially as we were all piled into the coach to be taken home.

As to be expected, I was a sorry sight in my damp clothes and sodden, ruined sandals. My mother gave me a good telling off and demanded to know how I had got into such a state. I said that I had slipped and fell into the water. The following day we had a caller - a journalist from the local paper. Somehow they had heard of the event. My mother was flabbergasted to hear what had really happened, and when the reporter left she asked why I had not told her. My answer and logic were simple: what I did was not important, but the sandals were. That week, the paper was published which caused me more embarrassment with a front-page headline, *They're All Proud of Heroine Jenny*. My school made a thing of it, the church mentioned it in their service and magazine and people kept stopping me in the street. For one so young, it was all too much and I sobbed my heart out only wishing to be left alone. I never knew where the child lived or what happened to him, but the memory of the day – and the sandals! - has always stayed with me.

The closest pub to us was The Enterprise and this was my father's local. The brewers usually owned pubs and, if memory serves, this was a Watney pub. Their distribution depot was based in Victoria, and it was not an unusual sight to see a large cart loaded with wooden beer barrels being drawn by two enormous dray horses. Most pubs had access to their cellars by wooden double doors set into the pavement or wall outside the pub. Here the barrels would be offloaded and rolled down a plank into the cellar. Wine was not even considered so the usual tipple was beer. Women rarely drank beer but a shandy was acceptable. My mother was rather partial to gin and orange, a sweet green liqueur called Green Goddess or a Babycham. Smith's Crisps were popular, and the salt was in a small twist of blue paper inside the bag. There were two bars, the public bar that was not as comfortable as the saloon bar where the drinks cost more. Should women enter the pub alone it was generally the saloon bar that she chose. Men usually preferred the public one, as it was here that they could play darts or dominoes. Under no circumstances could children enter a bar, so should the adults wish for a drink, the children would be left outside with a glass of lemonade and a packet of crisps or sometimes a large flat dry arrowroot biscuit. It was a meeting place for the locals and it met many of their needs, with a Christmas Club where a set sum a week could be collected and saved for the next Christmas. Loans were also possible should extra money be needed.

A trip to the seaside, but a rather unconventional donkey ride

An annual coach trip to the seaside was a highlight of those post-war years. Before setting off, beer would be loaded into the back of the coach and one of the tyres chalked with numbers starting at one. When the coach arrived at its destination the person holding the number where the wheel had stopped on the ground would win a prize. The beer was enjoyed at the natural break stop on the way out and on the way back. Sometimes a meal would be organised at a local restaurant. Everyone always enjoyed the day with the funfair and beach. Paper hats were in, and bonnets flaunted a message, the most popular being *Kiss Me Quick*. Even though we were only away for a day, saucy postcards, or those with a view, were always sought and then sent off to friends and family.

Most ordinary families were not wealthy. After World War I there were depressions in the 1920s and 1930s, followed by World War II which led to shortages even into the early 1950s. Most people lived in rented accommodation and held a rent book. Each week the "rent man" would call to collect the sum and enter it into the rent book. If anyone had to prove that they were good regular payers, this would be the one thing to produce as evidence. Should anyone get into arrears, they could pay an agreed extra amount, which would be paid until the debt was cleared. Insurance against death was a must for many and another regular weekly caller would be the "insurance man". Yet again, there would be a book to enter the payment. Often this would be for pennies rather than shillings. An older friend in 1993 received £400 on the death of her husband, having paid two pennies or the equivalent per week over 50 years. Yet another regular caller could be the "Provident man". He would give the householder a cheque for a sum and this could be used at selected stores to buy goods. Once again, it was paid back on a weekly basis. Everyone dealt in cash. A bank account was uncommon and credit cards unknown. A common ruse of the day was to send a child in the family to the door and instruct him or her to say to the caller: "Mum's out." He was wise to such tricks and would say something like: "I'll give you a penny if you can tell me what time she'll be home." In all innocence, the child would turn round and call: "What time will you be home, mum?"

My photo souvenir from the wonderful Festival of Britain, 1951

Few people had a camera so it was usual in the streets of London and elsewhere for a photographer to take a photo as you walked along and press a card into your hand to get a sale. At the seaside, they would be forever present and some had their own pitch with large toys on which to sit or tall wooden structures on which pictures of fat ladies and men were painted without their heads. Instead there were holes where the person being photographed would face. For formal photographs, one would visit a photographer's studio. Photo machines were not in existence, and the first time I saw one was at the Festival of Britain.

Clothes were in short supply and coupons limited. Thus, many older garments were unstitched and remade into a new style or cut down for children. Certainly, it seemed to me that all my clothes were forever exceptionally long at the start and then as I grew and grew they got shorter and shorter. I recall being mortified when I was confirmed. Fabric was in short supply and clothes rationed, so it was back to being resourceful. My confirmation dress was made of parachute silk. It sounds wonderful but was in pink and white rather than all-white. Many children had white dresses so I really felt awful, but my mother never knew as I realised how hard she had worked to make me the dress.

The future Queen Elizabeth and her sister were youngsters and often dressed in the same style. Mothers often tried to emulate them with their own children. Bows for the hair and short ankle socks which I endured with the horrid white mark from their existence being on my ankles for years. Adult women wore stockings, and silk was rare – but brown colouring was not. Many women painted their legs brown to simulate stockings, and those who were more adventurous managed to draw a seam line up the back of each leg.

Schoolgirls had the dubious joy of having to wear fleecy, lined, loose black knickers with elastic around the waist and legs. They even had a pocket in the front of one of the legs in which to put a handkerchief! Many women wore corsets with bones to hold the shape of the figure and hooks and eyes running from the top to the bottom of the garment to hold everything in place. Fortunately, by the time I left college, these were not the norm for younger people. Instead, we wore roll-ons: an elasticated tube which we pulled up from the floor and, with plenty of wriggling, pulled into place over the hips, stomach and bottom. Suspenders were an integral part and these were then clipped onto the top of stockings. The garment was hot and tight to wear. An improvement came when a company called Playtex produced a lightweight "rubber" roll-on. Nevertheless, the wriggling to get it on and off was a normal part of the day. Liberation came years later when tights were introduced.

At 11 years of age, we had to take an entrance exam for our next school. The goal was to attend a grammar school. I passed to go to Buckingham Gate Grammar. However, there was only one place, and two children. An interview was needed. My father took me, which was the only time in my life that he attended anything to do with my schooling. He spent most of the time enthralling the females on the panel (I have mentioned that he was handsome and charming) and then proceeded to say that I was difficult to control and would only do what I wanted to do. Bearing in mind that as he had been in the army for six years in the war, he really did not know me. The result being, I lost the place at the grammar school and went to a general school, Chelsea Central Secondary Modern, based in Parsons Green. It was rough and tough. Fortunately, I was able to take another exam to apply for a technical college.

At the age of 12, I left my school and started at the all-girls' Wandsworth Technical College, where I excelled for the next three years. In my final year, I became Head Girl. We followed all the usual lessons, plus cookery and needlework. Everyone had to wear a uniform and a rather strange-shaped beret. It was all very ladylike and the emphasis was always on correct behaviour. Our school was on the top floor. Both morning and evening, a teacher would be standing at the top. Always, it was required to greet the teacher and she in turn would acknowledge each of us by name.

Lunchtime was an important part of the day. We sat at long tables which had been laid by the students. Each week, a different teacher would sit at the head of each table. The girls took it in turn to sit to her left and right. It was instilled in us that it was our duty to make polite conversation with her and the other students. Never did we help ourselves from the dishes, but always offered to others first and asked another student to pass water, salt, pepper or some other dish. Throughout, we were watched to ensure that we were holding our cutlery properly, had elbows close to our bodies, used our napkins correctly, etc.

I was keen on sport and good at it. One day, we had an away netball match in another part of London. That evening, my mother was taking me to the London Palladium to see a variety show. We were to meet at Oxford Circus. I was late, and on arrival she was not there. For some reason, I thought that I should walk to Tottenham Court Road to see if I could find her. I did not succeed, so I retraced my steps to the original meeting spot. However, I was now aware of being followed by a man. So, back I went to Tottenham Court Road where I had seen a policeman earlier. I approached him and explained what had happened.

At that time there were blue police boxes at various points along streets with a light on the top and a phone. The light started flashing, and the policeman answered the phone. He turned to me and said: "Is your name Jenny Emmerson?" He then said that the police were looking for me and he would take me to the police station where my mother would come to meet me.

At the station, I was given hot chocolate and waited. It had all come about when my mother returned home, hoping that I was there. Not finding me, she went to Chelsea police station armed with photos. The police then alerted the West End stations and I was saved!

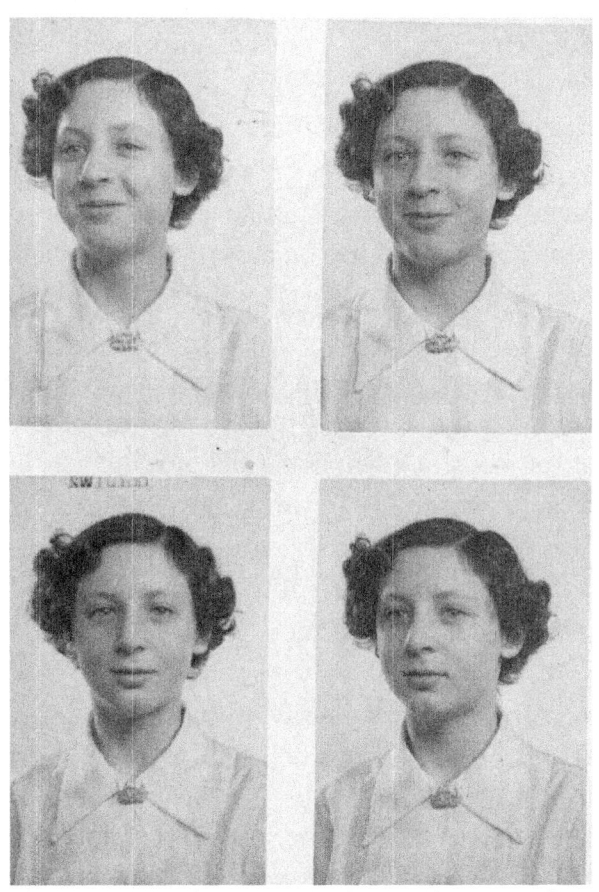

The passport photos my mother used to alert the police of my appearance

To get to my college I had to take a bus from Chelsea to Clapham Junction and then another to Wandsworth. Coming home one wet, grey late afternoon, I got on the bus at Clapham Junction and climbed the stairs to the top deck. The air was damp, the windows misted and running with condensation, and it was dark outside, with the shop lights reflecting onto the wet pavements - typical winter weather. There was only one seat so I sat next to a man reading his newspaper. I then became aware that he had moved the paper and was exposing himself. Each time a passenger moved past he dropped the paper over his lap. As soon as a seat became vacant, I moved to it. Although I was not sure what to do, I made a mental note of his dress. When the bus stopped at Oakley Street, I jumped off even though it was a fairly long distance from home. I ran and ran. On arrival, I collapsed in tears. Mother, as per usual, dealt with it and the police were contacted. They said that they would be putting police on the route. With my description, he was caught. I was asked to attend court but my mother would not allow it. I never heard any more.

6 POWERING ON

On holiday in Guernsey, about the time I started working at the London Electricity Board

Before I left Wandsworth Technical College, the Chief Engineer of the London Electricity Board, South Western District, approached the Headmistress seeking a final-year student for a possible job opportunity. She recommended me. Having had an interview, I was told that I would be accepted, providing I passed the medical with the company doctor. I attended alone and it was not until years later that I realised that his examination was more than cursory. I remember feeling uneasy at the time but, being totally innocent, assumed all was normal. Added to which, I really wanted the job. And so it was, in the summer of 1955, that I started work as a trainee at the London Electricity Board's Wandsworth showroom. It was a small shop with a manager, a cashier and me. Upstairs was the electricians' department, where the electricians would come in daily for their work. I was told that under no circumstances should I answer the telephone or speak to members of the public. The job would eventually lead to being a demonstrator, but I would have to start as a trainee and take both day-release courses and night school to obtain further qualifications, including electrical ones. I had to dust all the appliances and often would be sent into a filthy basement to do the filing. The most glamorous end of the job this most certainly was not.

The manager was horrid, and very rude. The cashier, Pam, was ten years older than me, and was very protective. We also used to have a Hoover representative calling in to pick up sales leads, and he would chat to Pam but was also very kind to me. I did not realise at the time that he was her boyfriend. I earned something like £2 per week, so with my first pay packet I bought a table lamp for my mother, which I still have in use over 60 years later. What I can say about this time is that I gained valuable experience relating to many aspects of direct contact with the public and those in education including complaints, accounts, selling, demonstrating and advising. It set me up well for my career that was to follow.

The lamp I bought for my mother with my first-ever pay packet

The dreadful manager bullied me continually, and it was nearly a year before I told my mother of my difficulties. I felt that as I was a working girl I had to stand on my own two feet, thus it was up to me to deal with things. However, once I had exposed him for what he was, my mother insisted that she would speak with the Senior Engineer (who, tragically, was killed in a plane crash some years later). I was promptly moved to the main showroom in Battersea.

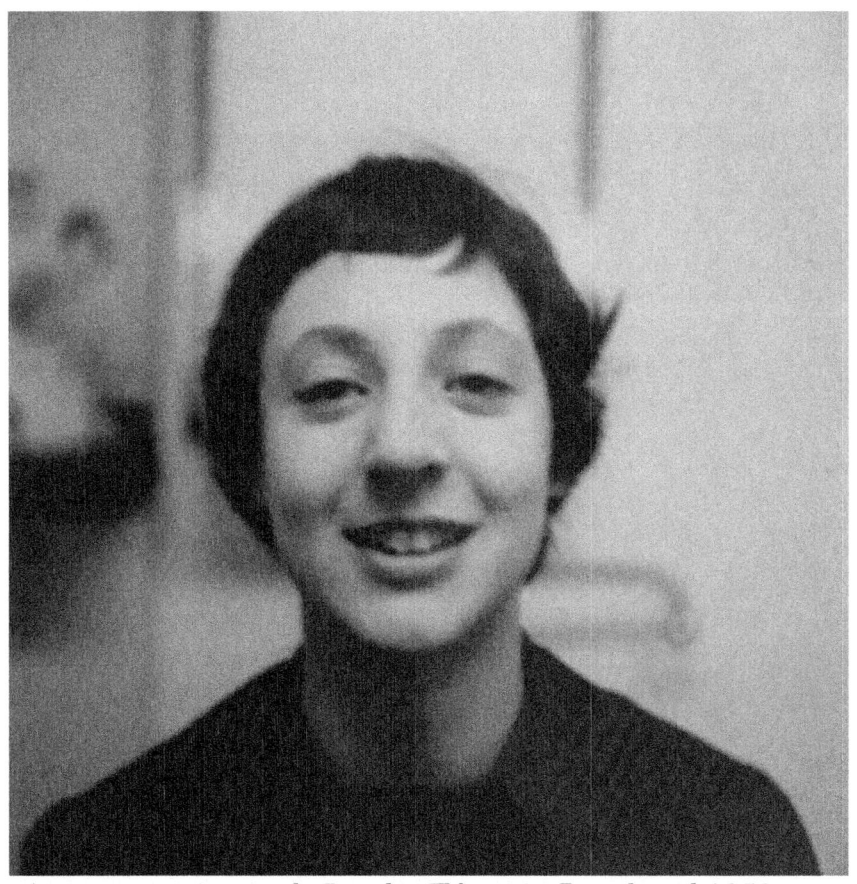

As a young trainee at the London Electricity Board, mid-1950s

One of the electricians in particular was always hanging around: Brian, who, a few years later, would become my husband of over 30 years. He told me later that he decided he would marry me, and over the following period accepted that he would be around, but would be one of many boyfriends I had. Meanwhile, Pam suggested that I go with her on a weekly basis to the Streatham Locarno, a dance ballroom. This I did, and continued to do so until after I was married. It was Pam, ten years my senior, who introduced me to this exciting new aspect of life. Every Friday night for most of the 1950s this is where we would be. At the end of the evening, we would always take a bus back to her family home, where I would stay over.

During my dancing heyday

On one occasion, Pam and I had been dancing all evening with two new male friends. They had a car, which was very rare for the time. They invited us to their flat for coffee and said that they would drive us back to Pam's parents' house. We accepted. Pam was on the settee with one fellow and, being me, I said that I would help with the coffee. Not a good idea: he ended up chasing me around the kitchen table! He cornered me and, although I managed to elude him, it remained with me for years, that feeling of being cornered. Needless to say, this was the last time we went back to a man's flat afterwards.

Brian and I became engaged during the late 1950s. He did

not dance, but he would take me to the Locarno and go to the cinema whilst I danced the night away, then would meet me to escort me home. I loved my nights at the Locarno, and I really enjoyed dancing and meeting people. At that time, my favourite drink was tomato juice. We entered at street level and the ladies' cloakroom was on the same level. From here, one could walk onto a balcony which encircled the ballroom below. This was good for viewing but not if one wanted to dance. By taking the stairs down, one entered the ballroom. A glass globe was fitted high into the ceiling which revolved and sparkled from any lighting. Small tables and chairs were scattered around the edge of a huge circular dancefloor and, on the stage, a live band played the music. There must have been at least 20 musicians. At one end was a long bar where the boys could drink and observe their prey. Most girls sat at the tables. When the music started, a boy would come, if one was lucky, and ask for a dance. Each dance session was three in succession, for example, three waltzes, foxtrots, quicksteps or rock numbers. However, if a boy was refused, the girl would then have to refuse all others until the next group of dances. I was quite lucky, and sitting out was not something that happened often.

All the girls dressed for the evening in their finery. It was fashionable to have layers of petticoats. A new idea to overcome the many layers was a contraption: a tape went around the waist and several went from here to about 12 inches above the skirt line. Here, there was a hoop which supported a ring of fabric. The last occasion I wore it: I was a keen dancer so was always happy to be one of the first on the dance floor. We were doing our quickstep when I became aware of something dangling between my legs! I asked my partner to move to the side of the dancefloor. It was here that I discovered the hoop had become disengaged and I was dancing with wires hanging down, and my beautiful full skirt was looking rather limp.

Not many of my generation, even now, are comfortable talking about sex. However, I really think that it is interesting to hear views of the time. Sex was not a word used in the fifties. Sexual behaviour was not discussed amongst my peers and certainly not with parents. To have a child out of marriage was considered to be a terrible slight on the family and a great cause of local gossip. Should it occur and if there was sufficient money, the girl was sent away from home. Termination was illegal and there were many back-street abortions carried out. The pill only came into being in the late fifties, so risks were high. In a roundabout way, my mother indicated that such an event would cause my parents untold embarrassment. The way to ensure that this could never happen was to only kiss the man that you were to marry and only shake hands at the end of an evening after a date. I followed this to the letter. Odd, but perhaps interesting. I had loads of dates, and even five proposals of marriage before I was 21. Even prior to my marriage, my mother advised against the pill. She maintained that it could bring "problems" later in life.

And yet, I seemed to be able to win the attention of men, whether I was seeking it or not. One time, a young man said that he was in love with me, but I replied that I felt we should finish our friendship. He arrived at my parents' flat one night, in a distraught state and begging me to change my mind. He became hysterical, so much so that he threatened to commit suicide by drowning himself in the Thames. At this point my parents phoned his mother, and said that they would get him in a cab. This is what they did and explained to the driver that he was not allowed to get out until he reached his home. I never heard from him again.

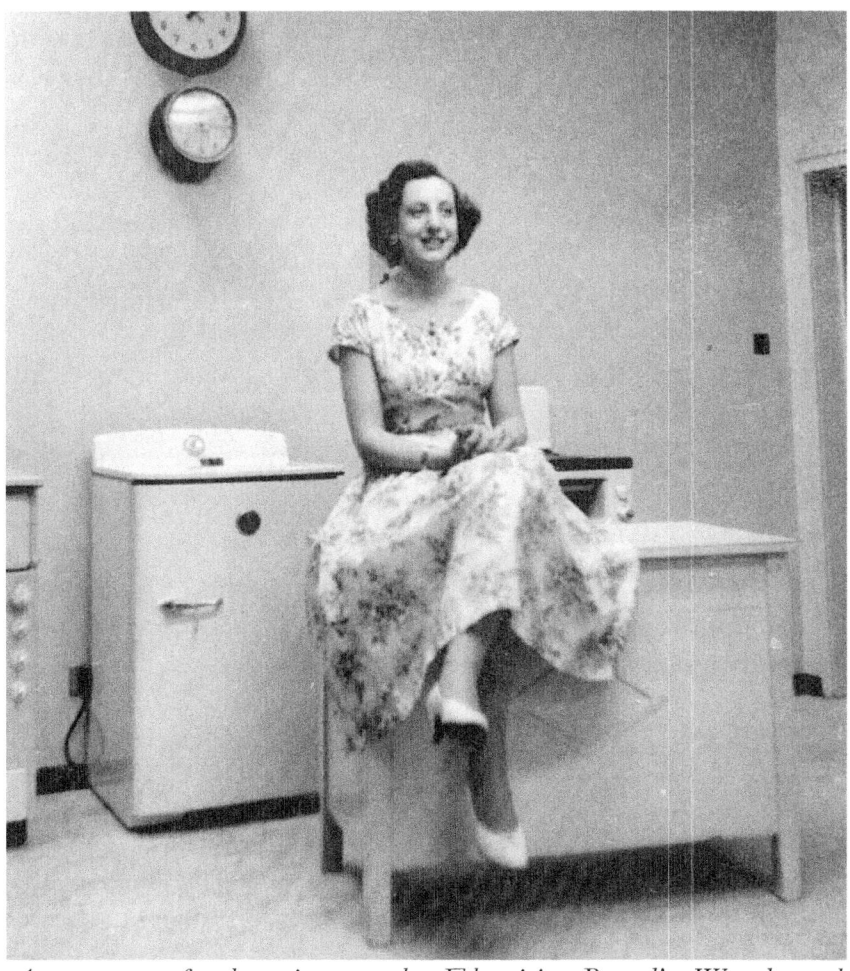

A moment of relaxation at the Electricity Board's Wandsworth showroom, 1950s

I didn't realise it at the time, but looking back now I can see that I was probably fairly attractive. Thinking back, my mother had told me when I was a little girl that I would never be pretty, but that I was *handsome*. Consequently, I always somehow felt inadequate. I would often end up on the receiving end of a chat-up line from men at the Locarno, and, years later, at work conferences or on trains and planes. I honestly wouldn't have a clue that I was being chatted up until I would recount the stories to friends later, who would enlighten me as to my male suitors' true intentions. I suppose this was a good thing really as it helped to protect me from getting hurt.

One of my regular dance partners at the Locarno was especially good. He invited me to attend a dance at the Aldwych. I think that the ballroom was called the Astoria. I accepted, but on the understanding that I was engaged and only going for the dancing. He had a car too, and at that time one could park nearby. We had a pleasant evening and went back to the car. Sitting inside, he put his arm behind my shoulders. At once I started: "I told you that I am engaged. I have had a lovely evening but that's where it ends!" He then said flatly: "Your door isn't closed." Oh dear, did I feel awful. I never saw him again.

In 1959, I left the London Electricity Board and I obtained a position as a Housecraft Adviser (later Senior Housecraft Adviser) with the General Electric Company (GEC), advising on and promoting the use of domestic electrical kitchen appliances. Then one day I was told that it had been arranged for me to give one week's live cooking demonstrations in the Electricity Board's prestigious flagship showroom in Regent Street in the heart of the West End! It was a seriously impressive place, with a huge plate-glass window looking into the street and, inside, a staircase made entirely out of glass leading to the upper floor. On arrival, I presented myself to the manager who was dressed in a morning suit. He then escorted me to the window where I would carry out my demonstrations. There waiting for me was a table, food mixer, electric cooker, all the utensils and all the foodstuffs. I had no choice but to get on with it.

Initially I was rather shy, and kept my head lowered especially when people gathered outside to view my efforts, so would pretend that I was unaware of them. However, it did not take more than a day for me to gain confidence. Soon, I was looking and smiling at the audience and, whatever I did, I found myself doing it with a flourish. Indeed, I became so confident and my viewing public grew so much that a policeman came into the showroom to ask me to stop, as I was causing congestion on the pavement.

Part of the role of a Housecraft Advisor was to judge local women's groups' cake-baking efforts. If it was a large organisation, there could be dozens of entries with the cakes proudly placed on white tablecloths over long trestle tables. This was not as easy as one would think, especially as the competitors would be standing in a group judging the judge with eagle eyes. To avoid excluding or ignoring any entry was vitally important, and so it was necessary to appear to treat every cake in the same manner.

Over time, I devised a judging system which eased the process of selecting a winner. Every cake had to be cut and tasted but immediately I could eliminate some just by looking, for example if the wrong size tin had been used, it had risen unevenly, the height was too low, had a cracked surface or was of an uneven colour. Even when cutting a slice, I could assess the cooked texture. On tasting, I could tell if an extra ingredient had been added to the given recipe, such as a flavouring essence or some grated peel. Over the years, ambition set in and I was also expected to judge decorated cakes, rock cakes, sweet and savoury scones and finally even homemade wine!

Having got used to the equipment and enjoying the "fame", I was on autopilot. One day, I was creaming butter and sugar together in the food mixer and once again giving it my all. However, I forgot to switch off the mixer, and lifted the beater head whilst the blade was still turning. This action caused the creaming mixture to be projected towards the window. Everybody outside instinctively ducked. I leant forward to scrape it off, and with an open gesture, shrugged my shoulders and mouthed: "It could happen to anyone!"

On one occasion, when I was demonstrating in the window of the Electricity Board's Hammersmith showroom in West London, a gentleman came in and said he wished to speak with me. He had an Australian accent and told me that he had a sheep farm at home, was comfortably off and that this was his last day before he returned to Australia. The purpose of his visit was to find a wife, and having seen me he felt that I would be suitable. As expected, I was taken by surprise as this was not in my job description. I thanked him for his kind offer and, showing him the engagement ring on my finger, said that I was already taken. He left rejected and dejected. Whether he succeeded in his mission on the way back to Heathrow Airport I shall never know.

One wet and windy late winter's afternoon, when everyone was well wrapped up against the weather, we were launching a new unique small square twin tub washing machine at the electricity showroom. It had a kidney-shaped tub and a spin dryer in the corner. It also incorporated a pump which would do away with the need to empty the water into a bucket. A couple asked me to explain to them the features of the appliance, so as it was connected to the electricity supply and water was in the tub, it was easy to demonstrate the special washing action and the method of emptying the water. To show how easy and simple this was, I placed the hose into a hole inside the top rear of the tub and explained that in their kitchen the other end of the hose would be placed into the sink. Once switched on, the water would then be pumped out via the hose. To illustrate the point, and as there was no sink nearby, I pointed the expelling water back into the tub. So enthusiastic about the machine was I that I continued talking as I switched the pump on. As I did so, the water gushed out of the machine and all over the poor couple: I had not realised that the hose was pointing squarely in their direction. The only thing I could think to say was: "What a good thing you are wearing your raincoats!"

I recall explaining to a young man how to operate a pop-up toaster, which he then purchased. However, he returned the next day to complain that it was not fit for purpose. When I examined it I saw that there was melted cheese in the area of the heating elements. On questioning him, he said that he had put the toaster on its side to make some cheese on toast. I explained that this was not the normal way of operating a toaster. He then complained, saying that the instruction leaflet should have warned the user not to carry out any other operation than toasting bread. Needless to say, he did not get his money back.

It was a typical winter's day, being a cold, dark, and wet Saturday afternoon when I was working in the Putney Electricity Board showroom. At that time the area was very upmarket and the showroom reflected this, with decor which included wood-panelled walls, and staff who were very attentive in assisting their clients.

It was almost closing time when a well-spoken, smartly dressed gentleman entered, asking to purchase a coal effect electric fire. As the junior member I was told to take him to the display area whilst the other staff were closing and locking up. He chose a model and rather than have it delivered after the weekend he wanted to take it with him. It was a bulky fire and as he had a car nearby he said that it would be easy to transport. Although by now it was well after closing, but as service was king, the manager said that we would wait and put the fire into his car.

We waited for his return, but eventually we left as it was likely that he had been delayed and would return on the Monday. At that time payment could be made by cash or cheque. He had paid by cheque, but never returned. Eventually the cheque bounced and his fire was returned to the stock cupboard. The lesson learned was, however, to always be helpful!

When I moved to the showroom, I was just 20 years old, and like many young people of the time, I was naive and learning more about the world. Not long after I started my new job, I was sent to Glasgow to attend an exhibition. The company made the arrangements for my transportation by train and booked me into the Ivanhoe Hotel for the required number of days. This was exciting as it was the first time that I had ever stayed in a hotel.

Me in full flow at a demonstration for the London Electricity Board in Brixton

On my arrival, I was impressed by its size, style, furnishings and the wide, long staircase leading down into the restaurant area. Shortly after going to my room and starting to unpack, I answered a knock on my door to a member of staff. Evidently, I had been allocated the wrong room and I would be taken to another. I was then taken some distance upstairs to an utmost floor where the corridor carpet seemed rather worn, and the lighting was dim. My new room was nothing like my original, and had a small window, a single bed and a tiny hand basin. There was no en-suite: the bathroom was along the corridor, which was not unusual in some establishments. By now it was late, and having had a long journey from London I was hungry but too shy to go to the dining room. The night in my dingy room was long, sleepless and I yearned to use the bathroom, but was frightened of entering the scary, uninviting corridor to get there.

In the morning, my boss was to meet with me at the hotel. As it was daylight I did manage to use the bathroom and walk down the staircase to order breakfast. This included my first taste of haggis (and ever since, it has been a food which I love). My boss, having seen my room, organised a change to one similar to my first, and from then, life, for me, was straightforward. However, over the years my thinking of that experience was that because of the exhibition, hotels in the city were fully booked. My second room would have been unacceptable to a more mature person, and because of my being so unworldly, I was the easiest person to move without fuss. Of course they were correct. Life lessons sometimes have to be learnt. From that day on, I always made sure I checked and supported any person younger than myself. I also learned that every haggis has a different taste and gets even better with a tot of whisky. This was also a time of change in my personal life. I had politely declined all the marriage proposals I had received, with the exception of Brian of course, and we tied the knot in August 1960.

Our wedding day in 1960

Alongside changes in my personal life as a young married woman, I also took the ongoing developments of my career in my stride. Part of my new role involved talking to school groups about electrical appliances and safety. As a part of the school curriculum in the late fifties and early sixties, teachers could take pupils to the major fuel companies to enhance their knowledge of kitchen appliances. To make it more interesting I was to give a lecture and demonstration of the capabilities of a range of electrical appliances to about 30-plus boys and girls with their teacher from a local school. I remember one such day vividly: the demonstration room was set up with a platform and seating. On the platform, all the appliances were on show, and some of them were connected to the electrical supply. I started by talking about the various appliances before giving a practical demonstration. At some point, a boy put his hand up, but as I wanted to complete this part of the session, I ignored him. He was persistent, however, and kept putting his hand up. Finally I asked him what he wanted. Without hesitation he said: "Miss, your cooker is on fire!" I turned to find black smoke wafting from the grill compartment! What had happened was that during my explanation of the dual-purpose grill, I had left the control in the "ON" position, so the element was still heating. I had forgotten to remove the instruction book from the grill pan and it was now charring, and well on its way to igniting. I was never one for cooking the books, and thankfully disaster was averted.

Out on the town, and with my trademark tomato juice, 1964

Post-war, the electrical industry was seeking to increase the use of electricity in the home. One asset for them was that the factories had stopped manufacturing arms and had returned to producing large electrical appliances such as cookers and washing machines. Part of the service for the buyer was to offer a home demonstration, and on one occasion I was asked to demonstrate a twin tub washing machine. As always, and being relatively young, I would try to dress the part to give the appearance of being older, knowledgeable and efficient. Thus, I wore a black suit, white blouse, a smart hat and the inevitable high heel shoes. Travel was either on foot or by public transport.

On arrival at the flat in the West End, I was taken by the lady of the house into the kitchen where another lady wearing a casual outfit was present. Having explained that any stain removal on collars or cuffs may need to be pre-treated, I then proceeded to explain the features and use of the washing machine whilst doing a white wash of her husband's shirts. On returning to the showroom I was chatting with another member of staff who told me that I had been with a well-known TV presenter and the editor of an upmarket magazine. However, there was no husband, and the shirts had belonged to one of the two friends. Another lesson learned early on: be careful and never make any assumptions.

The year 1966 was another period of change: Brian and I moved into our house early that year. It cost £5000, and our mortgage was £17 a month. We had been obliged to get a mortgage through the Greater London Council, as in those days it was frowned upon for a woman to be part of a mortgage application through a bank. Somewhat ironic, given that I was the principle bread-winner. It was also the year that I changed jobs, moving on to the next stage of my career, which would see me through to the late 1970s. When I moved to the Appliance Testing Laboratory in

Leatherhead, Surrey, I was hired to set up, and lead, a section dealing with the performance testing of electrical appliances. During this time, I worked both at home and abroad dealing with the formulation of specifications for appliance safety testing. I dealt closely with Area Electricity Boards around the UK, advising on the performance of appliances and giving lectures on performance testing, the latest technology and new developments at major trade and education conferences. I advised college and university lecturers on the principles of testing and how these could be incorporated into students' programmes of study. I got to work across the industry, with contacts ranging from government departments to appliance manufacturers and consumer organisations such as The Consumer Council and Association. Through my work, I instigated the approach of accepting college and university students at the Appliance Testing Laboratory for industrial practice.

This was a significant step up in terms of responsibility and seniority. I managed a team of five staff, and was responsible for the whole gamut of running the show, including administration of the testing section, budgeting and finances, managing and delivering the testing, report writing, the formulation of test specifications and liaising with manufacturers with respect to appliances or any disputes arising from the final test results. I was also responsible for supplying information to the Marketing Department and Press Office, and it was later on in this part of my career that I became involved in broadcast media and began to make radio appearances.

The electrical industry as a whole was very much aware of the importance of safety and performance of appliances, and no electricity company would sell any appliances unless and until they had been thoroughly tested at the laboratory for both safety and performance. All were required to conform to national specifications. If they did not, the manufacturer would have to go away, make necessary adjustments to meet the requirements and re-submit once they had put the objections right.

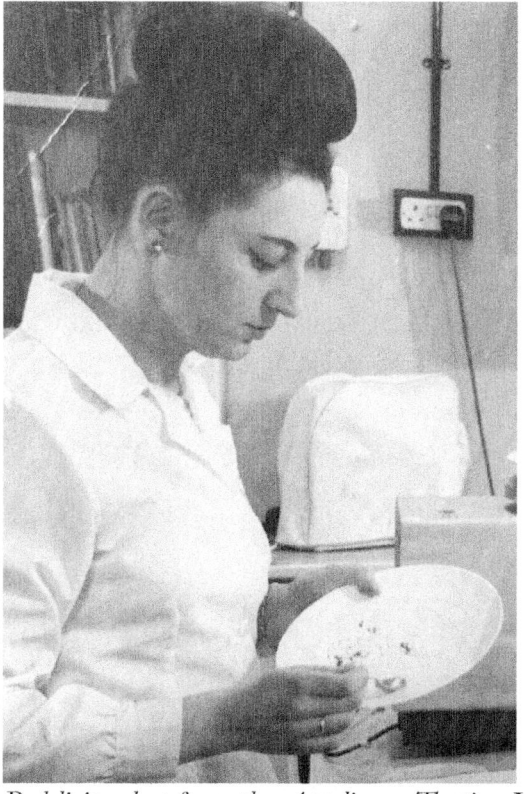

Publicity shot from the Appliance Testing Laboratories, 1966

The tests we devised and carried out were as diverse as the range of products we had to test. We dropped electric irons from specified heights, several hundred times, whilst electric blankets were run over with a large wooden roller 1000 times in each direction. We also had specific tests for washing machine effectiveness. Special fabrics were impregnated with blood, grass stains, tea and the like. After washing, we used a special reflectometer to assess cleaning results. As time went on, the appliances changed and diversified. When microwaves started to become available, we developed a test to check microwave leakage (there was a defined maximum allowance of 5mW per square centimetre). Appliance doors would be opened and closed hundreds of times. Safety and good working order were paramount, and each appliance had to be tested, approved and properly documented to ensure no dangerous or substandard products were released to the public. Many years later, after my retirement, I was thrilled to receive a Distinguished Service Certificate from the British Standards Institution (BSI), awarded to me "in appreciation of long and valued contributions to the development of British, European and International standards".

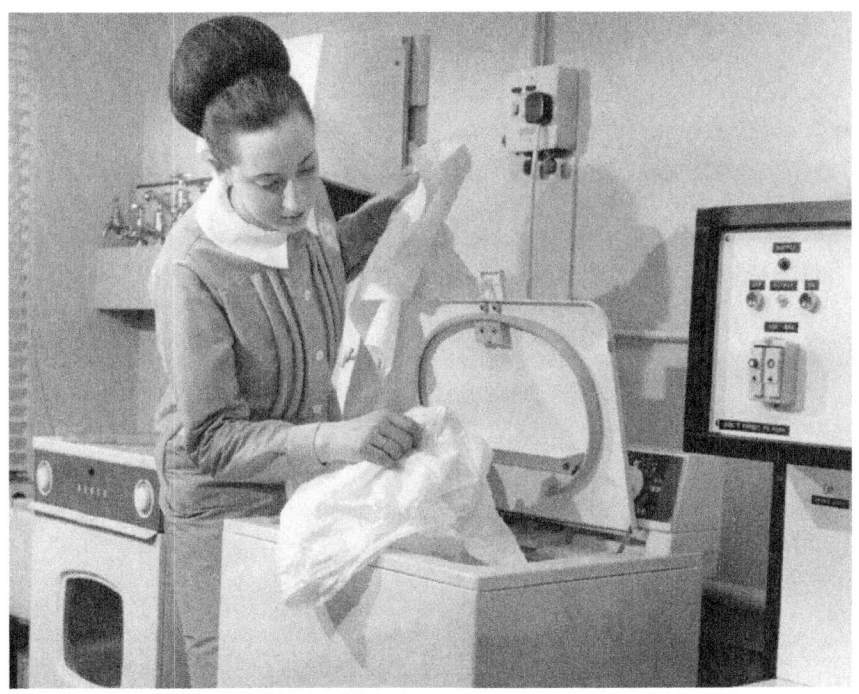

Testing washing machines, 1966

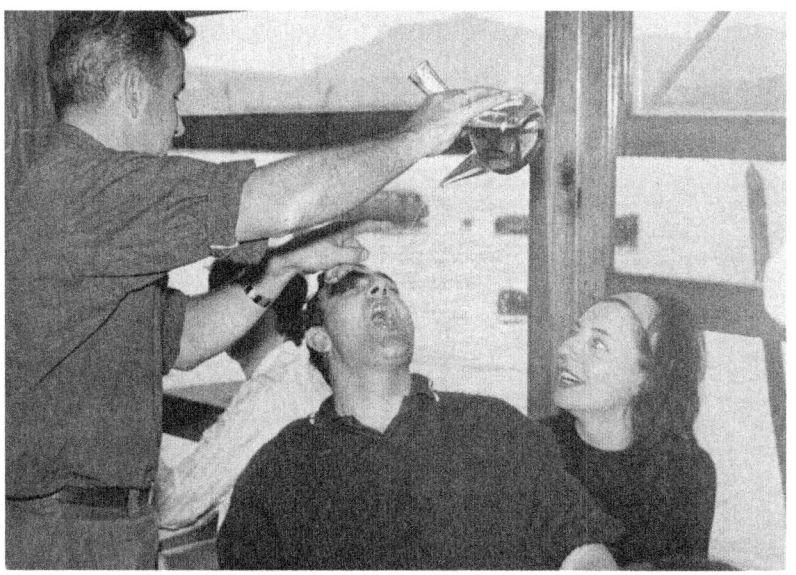

Brian and I on holiday in San Sebastián – and enjoying the local sangria – 1960s

Beyond the laboratories, external networking was a large part of my job. I represented the UK on the various International Electrotechnical Committees (IECs) which were developing both national and international standards specifications for the testing of domestic electrical appliances. International meetings were part and parcel of this, and an aspect of the job that I loved. When the Equal Pay Act went through Parliament in 1970, it paved the way, eventually, for men and women to be entitled – in theory at least – to receive the same pay for the same work, even though it would only come into force some five years later. I was the only female group leader at the testing laboratory. All my male peers were on a higher salary than I was, yet I was the one doing all of the international work as well, representing the UK industry abroad. One day I went to my boss to ask for a pay rise to put me on a level playing field with my male co-workers. He turned me down flat. When I asked why, he responded:

"Because you're not an engineer." In spite of showing him that my experience and qualifications were equivalent to engineer level, he would not be persuaded.

Many years later, when he was a guest of mine and Brian's for his retirement, he admitted to me that he had been wrong to refuse me the rise. By that stage, there had been a lot of water under the bridge, and my career had progressed in other ways.

7 OUR WOMAN IN RUSSIA

Part of the international delegation in Leningrad, Russia, 1971

My international work took me to many places throughout the world, including the Communist-run Eastern Bloc countries. Although there are plenty of happenings from that period, the most memorable was attending an international meeting on testing standards in Leningrad (now Saint Petersburg), Russia, in 1971. Unlike other times when I travelled overseas representing the UK, I received briefing documentation in advance from one of the British government departments. This contained both advice and instructions regarding my forthcoming travel and stay in Russia. It covered numerous aspects, such as use a UK airline, be aware that hidden microphones would be used everywhere including in the conference rooms, and within the hotel rooms surveillance cameras were also likely to be installed. Other advice given was that if one was *indiscreet* whilst away then this activity would be reported to UK police on returning home. I would add that as I was the only female representative (at the time it was very unusual to have a woman involved in an event such as this) the documentation seemed to be addressed entirely towards men! Much more was included, but at that time in the UK such activities to us, the general public, were unknown, added to which, it also included instructions to dispose of the documentation after reading it. Very cloak and dagger! It was most disconcerting and felt rather like I was going into a very different world: one of subterfuge and espionage.

Flying directly into Leningrad by a British carrier was not possible at that time. Thus, I flew BA from Heathrow to Warsaw, where I had to change onto an Aeroflot flight. There I sat in a public waiting area which was overlooked by a balcony where armed personnel were circling and observing. This caused me concern, as I had never seen people like this in London at the time. Thankfully I had taken a magazine to occupy myself so I took it out to read, trying to appear relaxed and nonchalant. With a start, I discovered that I was holding it upside-down! Fortunately, after some while, I was joined by two other delegates, one from Holland and another from France, a well-built chap who, it turned out, had been in the resistance during the war.

Eventually the aeroplane arrived and we boarded along with other passengers. They appeared to be Russian and with baggage which seemed to be more appropriate for travelling by horse and cart. An air hostess offered me a boiled sweet to suck on for take-off. The plane was really old and tatty, and during the flight its rattling was very noisy, not to mention rather worrying.

Leningrad Airport turned out to be rather surprising after Heathrow and other world airports. It was in an isolated area with a very small building, all of which had an air of drab sadness about it. Having trudged to the building from the plane, we queued in a narrow corridor in single file for our passport check. Here a rather grim-faced officer sat behind a screen and I felt most unnerved by the time I reached the counter to be inspected. The next small room was for the luggage collection, and by the time we got there the locals had mainly gone. Meanwhile we were filling in a declaration form which demanded to know how much foreign currency and jewellery we were carrying, amongst many other questions. By now the room was empty and our luggage had still not arrived. We were eventually informed it had not been loaded onto the plane. My French colleague would not be fobbed off, pointing out that we had journeyed from three different countries, so the explanation didn't hold water. Eventually the cases arrived but had obviously been searched, as my flimsy nightwear was peeking out from my closed case.

Finally, as the only three passengers left in the building, we moved to another holding area where an armed Russian-speaking customs officer demanded to know what I was carrying. The "conversation" was difficult and, on my part, worrying. It went as follows: I said I was carrying papers, and he demanded to know what sort. I said meeting papers and magazines. Eventually he allowed me to leave and join the other two. Later I was told that certain books and magazines, including the Bible, were forbidden to be brought into the country.

Hours later, the whole building was deserted save for us. With no Roubles (as the money exchange booth was closed) and no transport visible, we appeared to be stranded in the middle of nowhere. After a search we found some sort of official and he arranged for a car to transport us to our hotel. The hotel was tall with an impressive, long flight of steps leading to the entrance. On entering, the view was that of an enormous floor area which at the furthest end accommodated the reception desk. On either side of the long walk were small tables and chairs which resembled the utilitarian furniture and decor of those found in the UK after the war. Having queued to register, the receptionist took my return air ticket and passport, neither of which I would see again until I was leaving Russia. It was here that I realised that all the hotel guests were delegates attending the various committee meetings and all had had no other choice of hotel.

From here, I took one of the many lifts with a 24-hour attendant to my accommodation which was above the third floor. I later discovered that the third floor could not be accessed as this was where all the spying equipment was carrying out its clandestine business. On exiting the lift to get to my room I noticed there was a desk in the centre of the corridor. I later learnt that this was also manned 24-hours. The person on duty was there to record the comings and goings of any person entering any room. My room was basic, but at least it had a bathroom attached. The only complimentary item was a piece of yellow soap less than two inches square. Added to which I had brought a sink stopper with me as I had been advised they were not always supplied.

The various committee meetings were held in different buildings throughout Leningrad, the majority being very palatial, having been built and used by past royal families. Most of the delegates travelled around by metro. At that time I had not experienced accessing a gate by placing the ticket in a slot (this opened a waist-high door on either side). On one occasion I did not follow the system and as a consequence, the door gripped me and would not open to let me through until I placed the ticket in the appropriate slot. The general atmosphere of the streets was reminiscent of London after the war, everything was drab and grey and devoid of colour. Huge advertisement boards praised the workers. As it was winter, even the local people, although well wrapped in dark attire, looked pinched and cold. Incidentally, I had been warned not to give or sell any clothing, especially jeans or nylons, as this would cause me problems with the police.

One evening we were treated to a ballet which was excellent, although we had to go and return in pre-arranged taxis, including one which had rust holes in the floor. On another occasion we were taken to the famous Hermitage Museum. This was really special and a wonderful experience, especially as it was only open for delegates. Earlier I had become aware that during the conducted tour a strange man had joined us. I was sure that he was there to keep an eye on everyone in the group. As I wanted to see if this was the case I made my decision. I decided I wanted to stay back as if interested in some specific artefacts with another member of the British delegation. All it proved was that we ended up getting left behind and lost! We finally found our way to the others and I learned a lesson to behave, especially in such a country as this.

At the end of all such international meetings, the host country arranges some form of reception or entertainment for all the delegates and their wives. On this occasion, we were invited to an evening reception at Yusupov's Palace, where in a large beautiful room with a ballroom attached, an orchestra played. Tables were laden with food and drinks including large quantities of vodka. There were only a few seats around so most had to stand for what turned out to be a very long time, especially as our hosts gave rather long speeches repeated in several languages. Meantime, rather a lot of vodka shots was being consumed by the nearby Russians who were insisting that I kept toasting with each of them. I was rather concerned about this as I was aware that I did not wish to insult the hosting delegates. Fortunately, I managed to conceal the glass in my hand and pretended to drink. I then passed this to a Canadian delegate to dispose of it, and then accepted the next glass and continued in this manner until I had acknowledged every one of their group.

The ballroom had a smallish dance floor and, nearby, an impressive flight of stairs leading to a balcony. Once the orchestra started playing I danced with a number of delegates and then was approached by a "merry" Russian who bowed, snapped his feet together and, in Russian, invited me to dance. Having accepted, he firmly took my elbow and guided me across the dancefloor and manoeuvred me up the stairs to the balcony where Russian men and women were congregating together. I soon realised that I was the only foreigner there. After my original dance there was no escape as I was receiving more requests to dance. Every time I asked if my partner spoke English or French, but with no success. Finally I managed to indicate to a partner that I wished to dance on the lower ballroom dance floor, and at last was able to return to the British delegates who had been wondering where I had been for so long. Shortly afterwards, the original Russian found me and tried to dance with me again. I refused and a British delegate led me onto the dance floor where the inebriated Russian proceeded to follow us around. Fortunately the music finished and it was time to depart but I was still being harassed.

Finally, the British delegation surrounded me and escorted me through the palace to the waiting coach with the man still in pursuit. The next day in the meeting room prior to the business discussion the same Russian approached me, bowed, snapped his feet together, spoke in Russian and presented me with a traditional red, black and gold decorated wooden spoon. That was the last I saw of him!

Doing my bit for international relations at a testing standards meeting in Greece, 1972

Later on in the 1970s, I became friends with a couple, Dana and Tony, in Prague, which at that point was part of the USSR. Over time, I heard much of the trials and tribulations of the family, which for me was a startling realisation of some of their horrific experiences. However, Dana was a singer with the then famous Linha Singers and Tony was working in other areas. On one of my visits, I was staying in their flat and early one morning Dana said that Tony wanted to cook a typical Czech dish and as he had heard that the required ingredient of a fresh cabbage was in a particular shop, he had gone out really early to ensure that he could get one.

He was gone all day and eventually returned both dejected and apologetic as, having trawled the streets, he never found a cabbage but did eventually manage to buy a jar of pickled cabbage. I felt so awful, as having just travelled from London, I could have supplied as many cabbages as they needed. It was a long time ago but to this day I have not forgotten their friendship and generosity of spirit.

Other foreign trips of that period were far less exotic and laced with intrigue, though equally interesting in their own ways. A French company wanted to import their kitchen appliances into the UK and sought advice with regard to performance testing required to access the UK market. As it was my area of expertise, it was agreed that I would visit them in Dijon for in-depth discussions, and they would arrange for all travel, accommodation and other expenses to be covered.

I flew into Paris from where I was driven for my overnight stay in the city centre to the famous 1928 art deco George V Hotel. The entry into my room had a small vestibule, and the room itself was beautiful with seemingly antique furniture. As one would expect in such luxury, I had a very comfortable and good night's sleep. The next morning, one of the company directors met me and we drove to an airport where his small light aircraft was ready and waiting for our take-off to Dijon. The pilot was not visible but it transpired it was my host who, I later learned, was an ex-fighter pilot. The flight was fascinating as I discovered more about his flying exploits, the plane and the manoeuvres we took en route, having a go at taking the controls, trying to keep the horizon level, and my dishy pilot swooping over a field full of cows. However, after our arrival I heard that he had been reported by the farmer who owned the cows, and I never heard the outcome. To this day I cannot remember the outcome of my business trip, but only the enjoyment of the hotel and plane ride.

Another French tale: I had won an opportunity to work for a number of weeks at the EDF (Electricité de France) laboratory. I could get by in French but I was not fluent, and I was excited and nervous, added to which I was to be alone for the first day. During the flight over I had a couple of G&Ts to calm myself in anticipation of what was the unknown. On arrival I went to the luggage hall to collect my case from the carousel. Gradually, everyone collected theirs but I just stood watching it going around and around with an unclaimed solitary case. Meanwhile, I was practising how I could explain in French the loss of my case. Suddenly, I had a eureka moment. The solitary case was mine, which I had not recognised because I had forgotten that I had bought a new one for my trip!

When I arrived at the hotel they informed me that they did not have a room for me and were unable to find me another one overnight as Paris was full of tourists. Eventually, an employee of EDF took me to his home where his family made me more than welcome. The next day I was settled into my hotel but having checked the price I realised that I had insufficient funds from my office to cover this and to pay for my breakfasts and dinners. I phoned home and asked Brian to send me some more money. Meanwhile, until it arrived, I had found a cheap bistro and had breakfasts of croissants and coffee, and dinners of either a cheese or ham toasted sandwich. Sometimes I was entertained for dinner which was a relief from my normal diet. The money never arrived because Brian was questioned as to why he wanted to send it abroad. We did not realise at the time that such action was not allowed. Finally the day came for me to pay the hotel bill only to be told that it had been paid! On reflection, I cannot understand why I did not phone my office but at the time I felt that I should deal with it myself. It sounds silly, but I still enjoyed the whole experience and it did leave me with yet another tale to tell.

I once went to Athens to attend a week-long specification meeting and the company had booked me into the best hotel in the city. After a successful event I signed out, asked the receptionist to arrange a car to take me to the airport and requested a porter to collect my luggage. When the car arrived, I sat in it to await the delivery of my luggage. It seemed an age arriving. Presently, the hotel manager appeared and, with apologies, asked that I return to the hotel as they had a problem. With him, I walked back through the hotel's large luxurious seating area to the reception desk. Here, it was explained why my luggage had not been delivered, and, to my horror, was asked to settle my account! I explained that my company had arranged my accommodation and expenses with the hotel and they were to be paid by them. Once more I waited for some time whilst a check was made, and, although I appeared relaxed and in control, I felt embarrassed and very uncomfortable. Finally, the manager returned, bowing and almost on his knees, and profusely apologised. The account had been paid in full and it was overlooked by a member of staff. I was then ushered out as if a VIP by the manager, and a porter and a chauffeur were standing ready to open the car door. The only thing that was missing was a red carpet.

Drama still followed me around on my assignments closer to home. One day in the mid-1970s I was asked to give a lecture at the North Eastern Electricity Board. Having friends in the north east, I spent the weekend beforehand at their home. On the Sunday they wanted to take the opportunity to show me Craster, a rugged but picturesque seaside village famous for its smoked kippers. However, the weather was horrific with lashing rain, gale-force winds and extreme cold. Having no clothes for such conditions, over my trouser suit they put on a heavy Aran sweater and a full-length one-piece waterproof boiler suit. Haute couture this was not, but it would do. My shoes had to remain, and were of a high block heel design with a retaining strap across the front of the ankle. On arrival we went to see the tiny harbour where the water within its walls was as rough and turbulent as the sea beyond. My host suggested that we took a walk along the side of the harbour wall to the entrance from the sea. Although nervous I agreed, but my girlfriend decided to stay on the shore. On my return I walked a few feet in front of my host. Suddenly from behind I was enveloped in water and thrust to the ground. Immediately, I was being tumbled back and forth towards the drop into the boiling sea, and the only thing stopping me from plunging in were the sleepers bordering the edges of the harbour. At last came a moment of calm and I was hoisted to my feet by my untouched host. We staggered to safety.

My friend had seen what was about to happen but had been

powerless to give any warning. She had seen an enormous freak wave coming towards the harbour, jump the seawall and strike the length of my back. She knew that once in the water I could not be saved as the weight of my outfit would drag me under and nothing could win against the conditions. The grit from the ground had torn through the waterproof suit, Aran jumper, suit jacket, blouse and leather gloves and had scuffed my shoes which had been only been held on because of the straps. It had also ripped a gold bracelet off my wrist. Later, I found that my feet were so swollen that I could only give my lecture the next day wearing slippers. My lecture was never reported but both the local radio and newspaper enjoyed my adventure and made some coverage out of it.

Immediately after my near-death experience in Craster, the first thing I did when getting back into my friends' car was to pull down the visor mirror to check if my make-up was still intact. I am happy to say it was. I did not tell Brian until I returned home, but much later, when we were using an automatic car wash, I suddenly burst into tears. It brought back the memory of the thundering and swooshing noise which I had experienced during my harbour encounter.

More shenanigans on another trip to the north. I was travelling by train in a first class compartment towards northern England where I was to give a lecture. Nearby was a young woman in a business suit with a young girl. I mused that she was in sales and the girl was her trainee. Part-way through the journey, we were informed that due to a train fault we would have to continue the journey by bus. As we joined the bus queue, the woman asked how much the fare would be as they had limited funds, so I reassured her that money would not be needed. However, we were then told to return to the platform as a replacement train was on its way. By now the travelling time had increased and the train had not arrived. The woman was in a panic as she explained that a friend was meeting her and so I said that this would be known at her arrival station. After another wait, she said that it was not a friend but a business colleague and she was very worried. This time I told her to go to the station master with the name and he could phone through with a message. She decided not to take up my idea.

Eventually our train arrived and they sat and chatted with me and even suggested that we meet up when back in London. Finally she said to the girl, "Shall we tell her?" to which she agreed. Now the surprise: the girl was her niece, and she was a friend of one of the perpetrators of the 1983 Brink's-Mat bullion robbery. It was he who had sent a visiting order and the money for first class travel, and it was the prison van that was to meet them at their station! Now that was an encounter which I am sure I will never forget. Sitting diagonally in a single compartment on the train journey back, a handsome well-dressed Frenchman was the only other occupant. When the ticket inspector arrived, the man enquired as to which Tube train to take on arrival in London. As he was unable to help, I offered to explain, and this led to us enjoying a general conversation until a restaurant member of staff came to enquire if we would be taking lunch, for which I had reserved a table.

In the restaurant car we placed our orders and whilst waiting, ordered gin and tonic. It was then that my French companion raised his glass and quietly said, "When I drink ze jin an' tonique, I am in lurve." Even though he knew that I was married, he then invited me to cancel my meeting in London and spend time with him at his hotel. I thanked him but confirmed that I would be leaving him to fend for himself when we got in to London. Once on the Tube, we sat on the long seats and I was aware of the curious looks we were getting from the passengers opposite. Eventually, as we were coming into my station, and as I said goodbye, he moved towards me to kiss me gently on both cheeks. In my confusion I got up with a start and promptly stumbled over his suitcase as I made my exit. To this day I am not sure whether to have been insulted or flattered by his suggestion!

On one assignment, I was in a UK hotel as I was to give a lecture the following morning and decided to have an early night. However, I was awoken by a fire alarm, but as I had recently attended a course on fire safety, I felt fairly nervous but also alert to the situation. I moved to the floor and crawled to the dressing table to get my jewellery and makeup bag, into the bathroom for a towel and back across the floor to the door. Using the towel around the handle I cautiously opened the door to find that the corridor was clear of smoke, and a few people were out of their rooms, asking what was happening. I suggested that they evacuate but not to use the lift. On going down the stairs, I kept to the wall and did not touch the handrail. The staff ushered us to an exit but said that as it was dark, cold and raining, we should wait inside for further instructions. Meanwhile, I thought I should put on some makeup as firemen were trooping through, and I was aware that some people were fully dressed and obviously were having a late night. Eventually, we were told that there was nothing to worry about as it was a false alarm. I returned to my room, and saw the time. It was only 9.30pm and I had only just gone off to sleep before the alarm sounded.

More adventures. I was to give a lecture one morning in Scotland and flew up the evening before. My hostess was to meet me at the airport and escort me to the hotel restaurant for dinner with invited guests. Unfortunately, my plane was delayed which was beyond my control, but even so, upon my arrival I apologised profusely. At the hotel, I said that I would meet everyone at the table but needed to change beforehand and would not be long. I rushed in and out of my room, and within minutes I was on my way in the lift going down to the ground floor. I was alone when suddenly it juddered to a halt. I pressed the down button but nothing happened so I rang the emergency line but there was no response. I repeated this several times and eventually after about ten minutes I was moving downwards. When the door opened, there was a member of staff outside and I complained about the lack of action. He then informed me that I had inadvertently used the staff lift and only a guest lift would be dealt with immediately.

At last I arrived red faced at the restaurant where a group of people were waiting at the table and yet again gave my apologies and an explanation. My hostess then introduced me to the guests, including the name of a young woman, adding that she was Gregory's Girl. I pondered for a moment and explained that I did not know a Gregory. Oh dear, once again I was embarrassed when I was told that *Gregory's Girl* was a recent and popular Scottish film. I can only say that it was not the most successful evening of my life.

Another time, I was in Aberdeen on business when a friend's elderly mother invited me to have a meal with the family. On meeting her, she was lovely and very welcoming, and she told me that she and her husband were not really townies having lived as farmhands until his retirement. Her stories were really interesting and enlightened me about another world of farm work, but as her accent was extremely strong and she spoke at high speed, I found it difficult to understand, so she kindly slowed down. However, after a short while she would forget, and I was left still struggling to appreciate all that she was saying.

I knew that she was a good cook and the high tea table was laden with homemade bread, preserves and cakes. Once seated, she told me not to stand on ceremony, and to help myself whilst she cooked a hot dish of fried crumbed fish. Once served, and wanting to be a good guest, I thought that a nice compliment to her would be to add some homemade chutney to the fish, and helped myself accordingly. She then quizzically looked at me and said: "*I see in London you take jam with your fish?*" My answer was no, but also added that both the fish with the jam was indeed very tasty. Once again, I had learned another lesson: to check before helping myself.

Drama just seems to follow me around sometimes. I had always wanted a mink coat, and when a friend informed me she could have one made abroad at a really low price, I asked her if she could get me a bespoke jacket. As soon as it arrived I decided to go into the West End as there were sales on and I really wanted to flaunt and show off my new acquisition. My final shop was the department store Selfridges, whose basement was teeming with chattering shoppers snapping up reduced china and glassware. I was looking at a tall display of lovely glassware, some of which I thought I would purchase. However, as I went to look at one of them, suddenly the whole display collapsed and with a huge noise fell, shattered and crashed onto the floor. For a few moments there was an eerie silence. I was frozen to the spot as an assistant rushed over and was worried to know if I was injured. I explained that I was just about to pick up a glass and without warning the whole display tumbled down and added that it may have been badly erected. She apologised profusely and said that she was relieved that I was unhurt, so I left her with the chaos. Actually, I was most embarrassed but thought that I should remain in the department to give the impression that I was relaxed about the situation. Thus, I continued to walk around, when what I was really aiming for was the lift. On reflection, at no point was I asked to pay for the damage and perhaps as I was not wearing an ordinary coat, my mink saved the day.

8 FRIDAY, 7 JULY 1978

Dinner

Pâté and Melba Toast

Coq au Vin
Beans, Mixed Vegetables and Rice

Sherry Trifle
Cheese
Coffee

Red Wine
White Wine

9 THE COOKING REVOLUTION

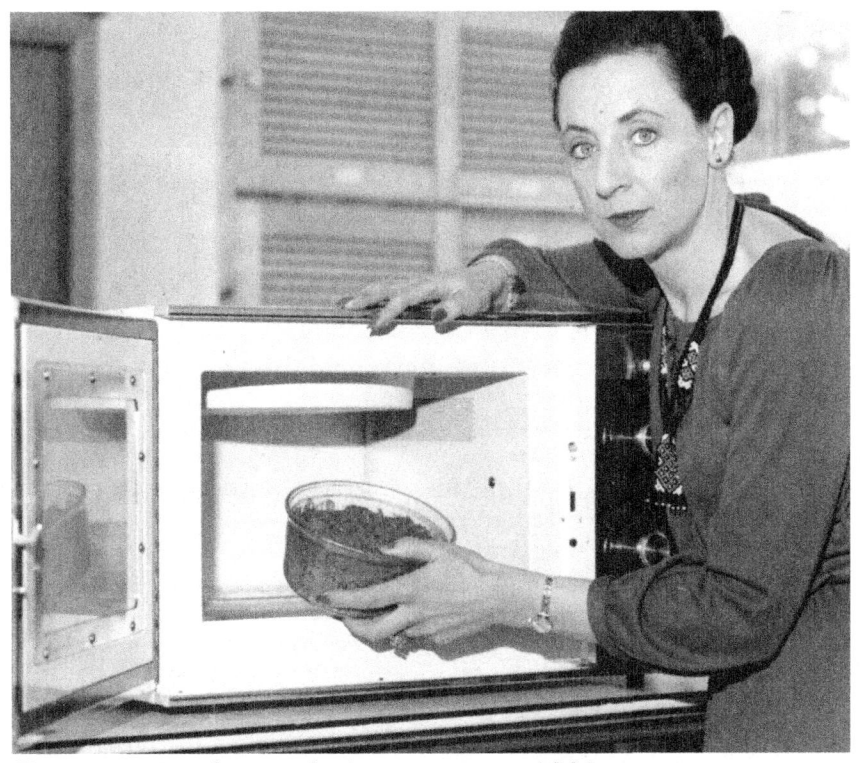

Demonstrating the use of microwave ovens, 1980

I can clearly remember seeing television for the first time and marvelling at the miracle I was witnessing. It was a wonderful mystery that fascinated everyone, and yet today nobody gives it a second thought. So when microwave cookers first appeared, they really did spark the same kind of interest. My first sight of a commercial microwave oven, an impressive machine called Artica, was at the Electricity Council Catering Centre in London, some time in the late 1960s. As time went on, I spent more time talking microwaves than anything else. At parties, general conversation was almost non-existent as

I answered questions from all directions on the new culinary technology. Microwave cookers simply were spectacular. My initial enthusiasm was based on loving the speed of it, its ability to thaw, heat or cook almost anything, the washing-up it reduced, the cleanliness of it and the electricity, and therefore money, I could save by using it. In time, via my books, magazines and radio and TV appearances, my job would be to guide budding microwave chefs to take their time to get used to the new techniques required. I always advised trying some simple operations at first: scrambled eggs, a jacket potato or just a quick cuppa.

In the very early days, I would typically be asked questions along the following lines:

Q. When you open the door, do the microwaves jump out?
A. No. As soon as the door is touched, the microwave energy stops - like switching off a light.

Q. Why must you pierce the skins of apples, potatoes and other foods?
A. As the food is heated, so the moisture turns to steam and must escape. If foods with a skin or membrane are not pricked, they may burst.

Q. Can I build my microwave cooker into my kitchen units?
A. In general yes, but do check and follow the manufacturer's instructions. Never cover the cooker vents and always leave a small air gap around the top and sides.

Q. How should you go about seasoning food before cooking it in the microwave?
A. Never sprinkle salt directly on to meat, fish or vegetables, as this can dehydrate and toughen the food.

Q. Why does it take nearly twice as long to cook two jacket potatoes as it does one?
A. One potato has the benefit of all the microwave energy; two potatoes have to share it.

At an early microwave power symposium held in Leuven, Belgium, I predicted that microwave ovens would never replace the conventional cooker, but would go on to find a place in the 1980s kitchen. I stated it was one of the few appliances which could be used throughout the world, without the need to alter the basic construction. Furthermore, it could be employed to suit the individual eating habits of whichever country in which it was to be used. The difficulty for manufacturers, I added, was to make the consumer understand that the oven works on a principle, something like the energy picked up by a TV. But rather than converting the energy into pictures and sound, energy waves for a microwave oven are at a different frequency and are directed into, and contained within, a small box – the oven – with the result that they shake up the moisture molecules in the food. The molecules then vibrate at an enormous speed and this creates friction which, in turn, creates the heat which cooks the food. Simples!

Published in the year of the Queen's Silver Jubilee in 1977, *Microwave – The Cooking Revolution* was the first in a long line of books I wrote about this new and very different appliance. At the time, being in charge of the Electricity Council's Appliance Testing Laboratories, I was well-placed to try and explain how microwaves worked, what they would and wouldn't do, and how to go about using one.

Sheila Black in *The Times* reckoned it was *"Well worth buying before you start shopping around for the ovens themselves."* Freezer

Family reported *"The book creates a greater understanding of the appliance and will enable the user to find joy in creative cooking."* Happily, the publishers Forbes were pleased with sales, so I followed it up with *The Microwave Cookbook* which appeared in 1978. My mission here was to explain and lead the cook through the special cooking techniques required and I boldly added in the introduction *"That way she will get the most out of her appliance and enjoy the speed and variety it suddenly brings to her cuisine. Or should we say 'or his' cuisine, since microwave cooking is specially appealing to men of any age?"* Research had shown that many men were regularly cooking for their family, and not just on special occasions. And unlike most cookery books from that distant era, the book's cover showed a pinafore wearing woman and man proudly displaying the dishes they had both cooked by microwave.

I set out the basics and general cooking information, including examples of what a microwave oven will do.

- Melt butter, chocolate, jellies and cheese
- Boil water, drinks and soups
- Soften butter, icings and frostings
- Roast poultry, game and meat
- Sauté meat and vegetables
- Casserole fish and meat dishes
- Bake some pastries, cakes and yeast mixtures
- Dry bread and flowers
- Steam suet dishes and fish
- Poach fish and eggs
- Heat/cook cold dishes
- Reheat/thaw frozen foods
- Toast nuts and desiccated coconut

This was all quite revolutionary for the 1970s – though I still wonder today whether all users fully appreciated the many ways the microwave could help out in the kitchen. I also included serving suggestions and pointed out whether dishes could be prepared in advance, and when best not to use the oven at all. The book featured 67 pages of specially written recipes. These ranged from hot spicy grapefruit and pizza to country casserole and bananas Grand Marnier. Retailing for a mere £1.50, the book would go on to reach its tenth impression by 1985, a testament to the growing popularity of cooking properly with a microwave. Fast-forward several decades, and you can imagine my surprise to receive a message some 40 years after the book was first published, via Twitter from a gentleman named Nick. He revealed that his pioneering grandma was still using my recipe for lettuce soup which he had just had for dinner. His verdict? "Absolutely delicious!"

In 1979, I was seconded to the Public Relations Department of the Electricity Council, at their headquarters in Millbank Tower, on the banks of the River Thames in Central London. This would eventually turn out to be the final stretch of my main career, and it would be here that I would stay until my retirement some 16 years later. This again was a marked change of direction in career terms. On a day-to-day basis I dealt with correspondence and telephone calls from the public, as well as with other sections of the Council's headquarters. I supported the work of the Home Economist in writing letters to the public which were the result of a massive industry-wide advertising campaign. I wrote appliance education sheets, provided the basic drafts for the books and became more closely involved in media relations and outreach. In 1981, I was made permanent, and I took up the role of National Home Economist in October of that year. With this step up, my work extended into new areas and at national levels to encourage any contact to think, buy, use or sell electricity and/or appliances effectively and efficiently. The work was diverse, challenging and rewarding. Daily responsibilities included dealing with telephone calls and correspondence advising the PR companies, education departments and food, textile, detergent and appliance manufacturers, as well as industry bodies and our own press office. I wrote a quarterly bulletin for Area Board Home Economists, where I also acted as judge for national competitions. I lectured and gave formal presentations on many aspects of electrical appliances, including energy efficiency, new technology, aids for the disabled, the latest appliance developments and running costs. On several occasions the audiences numbered 1000 people.

Me at an uncommonly clear desk at Millbank, early 1980s

I had always been an early riser, jumping into my two-tone red Ford Capri for the drive into Central London every morning. I had always dreamed of owning an E-Type Jaguar, but the Capri was the best I could manage, and I referred to it as a poor man's E-Type. Thus, throughout my adult working life I always drove this model. And I think it was sometimes the car, rather than me, that was the reason I was stopped a number of times by the police.

I was first halted in 1979 by a grey-haired policeman. He gave me such a dressing down and a very serious lecture as to why I should not exceed the speed limit. He said that it was a warning and he would be on the lookout for me. Certainly, it had the right effect, and for many years I drove within the limit on that particular road. The next time, I was driving to work along the Embankment in Central London early in the morning. Suddenly, a policeman, wearing his helmet, came from nowhere and indicated for me to stop. He then expressed surprise that a woman was driving and thought my car was a stolen vehicle, so I had to stand at the roadside, unable to leave, until he had checked my registration and confirmed that I was the owner

The final occasion occurred driving through Victoria near to the mainline station when two police officers indicated for me to pull over. This time, I was questioned in the car and then asked if I had anything in the boot. I said not, but that they were free to check. However, the policewoman said that I was to get out of the car and open it in front of them. Having done so, I was then told I could continue my journey without any explanation as to why I had been stopped in the first place. All very strange.

Police intervention or not, I was always stationed at my desk in Millbank by 7.30am. So I look back now and wonder: how did I ever find the time and energy to throw regular dinner parties at home in the evening, after a crunching day in the office? It was hard work, but my secret was to do a lot of the culinary preparation in advance. When my guests arrived, Brian would serve the drinks as they tucked into the canapés. These I would prepare the night before – perhaps small squares of fried bread piped with cream cheese and a small piece of tomato. I would also prepare a dish of stuffed olives, silver onions, gherkins and cheese cubes to be nibbled with the aid of wooden cocktail sticks.

I always prepared everything properly, aiming as I was to be a little bit upmarket. This encouraged my guests to dress up and behave accordingly. Men wore suits and ties, while the ladies were in evening dresses and heels. There was never any slacking. So you can imagine my horror the first time one of my guests turned up wearing a woolly jumper! This signalled a change in attitudes, ushering in a much more casual era in home entertaining.

A typical dinner party menu at the time would consist of prawn cocktail for the starter, with moussaka as the main dish. Baked Alaska was a regular favourite for dessert. Incidentally, I had a lot of fun recreating this very menu several decades later especially for the three-part series Tastes of the 70s on my YouTube channel, with my good friends Peter, Matt and Mike. We had such fun filming, cooking and generally fooling around, and I seem to recall we got through quite a lot of wine. I even donned evening dresses I had kept from that era!

In my role of National Home Economist, I wrote, broadcast

and lectured widely not just on cookers, but all domestic electrical appliances. I continued to help to develop the Council's testing specifications in conjunction with the IEC (International Electrotechnical Commission) and BSI, and I continued to advise the Home Economists of each of the various regional Electricity Boards. This was long before these were privatised in the 1990s, when familiar names like SWEB, LEB, SWALEC, MANWEB and SEEBOARD vanished from the High Street.

The wonders of the microwave oven became my particular area of expertise. Through my appliance testing years, I had gained in-depth knowledge of their ingenious technology and construction. Reading cookbooks from the United States helped me to familiarise myself with testing microwave oven techniques before I pioneered recipes for users in the UK through my books and magazine features, which ranged from the basics to more ambitious meals. Consumers soon cottoned on to the benefits of buying a microwave thanks to their versatility and their ability to cook in next to no time, whether boiling, baking, roasting or poaching. Joints could be roasted in minutes and snacks heated in seconds. Microwaves have always been excellent for defrosting and reheating frozen food, whilst reducing running costs since there is no need to pre-heat as with a conventional oven. And of course the public loved the fact that a microwave could be conveniently plugged in anywhere it was needed.

As cookery demonstrations had formed part of my early career, I found myself ideally-placed to help educate and inform the public as a spokesperson for the electricity industry. I also twice held the Chairmanship of the Microwave Technologies Association, which had been inaugurated a few years earlier in 1978.

At work at the Appliance Testing Laboratories, May 1978

10 MY MILLION-SELLER

Writing was a significant part of my job, and fortunately it was something I loved. From the early days at the Electricity Council I was pretty much given free rein to write what I wanted to in terms of books and magazines. During my time there, and throughout my time at the Appliance Testing Laboratories before it, I had meticulously kept books of clippings from my magazine articles, as well as newspaper coverage of my various exploits around the country. Without them, I would be powerless to share all manner of snippets from past decades with you now.

"Attractive housewife who leads a double life." No, this July 1971 headline didn't scream out from the *News of the World*, but the slightly less salacious *Swindon Advertiser*. *"At home she spends her time cooking, washing up, laundering her husband's shirts. At work, she spends her time, cooking, washing up, laundering."* Variations appeared in other regional papers: *"Why Jenny is tied to the kitchen sink"* was a headline enjoyed by readers in Barrow-in-Furness and South Shields, over a syndicated article about me working at the Appliance Testing Laboratories. *"Mrs Webb, who is head of the housecraft group, tests new cookers, dishwashers, food mixers and washing machines,"* it continued. *"Continental mixers, she says, aren't always suitable for use in this country. In most other countries, they are used for beating egg whites and whipping cream. Continental bread is lighter than ours, and fruitcake is unheard of. Therefore, the housewife can find the beaters too light when she buys a bargain mixer from abroad so she chucks the machine out saying 'Mixers are no good'."*

Another clipping reminds me that my idea for an electric bath cleaner won a prize at the Home Economics Awards. This must have been during one of Britain's periods of industrial strife as I helpfully explained to a reporter: *"Home economics can make a special contribution in the present economic situation where the conservation of fuel and food and a shortage of many basic materials is of prime importance."*

My job at the Leatherhead Appliance Testing Laboratories also brought me to the attention of the magazine industry. This was at a time when print editions were still highly profitable for their publishers, decades before the impact of the digital revolution. *Woman* was one of the top-sellers back in 1974, when I was asked to join their panel of household experts to respond to readers writing in. In May that year, I see that I didn't hold back in one of my replies: *"Every other day we hear of clever husbands and wives who monkey with electric appliances while the power is still on and electrocute themselves. Nobody but a qualified electrician should ever open up the 'works' of a washing machine."*

From 1978, I had begun writing regularly for *Home and Freezer Digest*. This handy compact-sized magazine is still fondly remembered by many cooks of that era. In my first issue, Mary Berry described how she used her new microwave in conjunction with her conventional cooker and freezer. Cue Jenny to explain how microwaves work with non-technical answers. Over the years, I shared plenty of themed recipes. My *Fast Soups* included cream of potato and thick vegetable soup, while a series on speedy suppers for two promised my *Hurry Curry*! And for Christmas, what else but a microwaved garland cake?

Meanwhile, the *Coventry Evening Telegraph* could hardly

contain itself in March 1979: *"Fast food is with us – and it's taken our breath away. Jenny Webb, Senior Home Economist for the Electricity Council, showed an audience of Coventry teachers how to do a baked apple in three-and-a-half minutes, a baked potato in eight minutes, a joint of beef in eight minutes and a one-egg chocolate cake in six minutes. Microwave cookers also make a saving on electricity. They use less than a one-bar electric fire and less than an electric kettle. They don't create excess steam, heat or cooking smells, so they may be used almost anywhere in the home. They cost from £180 to £500."* And as if that weren't enough, the paper also raised some of the surprising claims that people were making about them. *"Microwave cookers 'boil your blood, make men sterile and boil your kidneys'. Jenny Webb refuted them all."*

The fact of the matter is that the Electricity Council wasn't really that interested in selling microwave ovens in the early days. But interest slowly grew, driven in large part by the Electricity Boards. I began to get invited by various different regions around the country to give talks about how to use microwave ovens effectively and safely in the kitchen. That's really how I became heavily involved in promoting microwaves, and authoring more recipe books which were designed to tempt the public to buy, and then fully exploit, their microwave ovens. Manufacturers really welcomed this of course, as they had been trying to build up microwave demand in the UK as well as globally for some years.

Producing recipe books was a painstaking, arduous and rewarding process. Once I had managed to decide which recipes to include, I enjoyed writing my cookery books enormously, but it was a challenge to juggle this with my busy professional and social life. Holding down a full-time job in the electricity industry meant that I had to write the recipes at home during the evenings and at weekends in my kitchen. Here, I had to ensure that I worked with the recipes as far as possible under test conditions, and maintain a professional working environment.

I always used my own kitchen for testing all the countless recipes for the numerous books that I wrote. Having studied domestic science, I suppose the maxim I tried to live by is: it's not what you spend, but ultimately your organisational ability, which makes a kitchen work. I had started testing electrical appliances back in 1966, so it was little wonder my kitchen became very well stocked with them. Thirteen separate sockets allowed me to use my machines – including a food mixer and a food processor – safely and easily. I always tried to practise what I preached so my home is totally electric, having had the gas disconnected when we moved in. I made full use of the Economy 7 tariff. Plug-in automatic timers meant I was able to use my dishwasher and other appliances during cheaper, off-peak energy hours.

My kitchen had been upgraded over the years, but originally – like many folk – I had first opted for inexpensive self-assembly units from MFI. Founded in 1964, this had been one of the UK's largest suppliers of kitchens and were located in many retail parks, although sadly the firm went bust in 2008. The kitchen walls and ceiling were pine for many years, and the floor was vinyl for easy maintenance. The main working surface has the best view of the garden with everything I ever needed to hand. A built-in ceramic hob was later upgraded to halogen – plus a new microwave oven of course!

All my utensils and scales were placed on the wall, with baking dishes and ingredients in cupboards above and below the worktop, and herbs and spices within easy reach in a nearby drawer. The other side of the kitchen houses the sink and fridge, and an area for making drinks and snacks, so this is where the kettle, toaster, coffee machine and china reside. I always tried to capitalise on wall space, with hooks for pans and so on, which meant I could make the very best use of time and energy when concocting and making the many hundreds of recipes for my books and magazine articles.

I was initially approached by Octopus Books to write a wide-ranging book of recipes based around microwave cooking, designed to showcase the versatility of this new type of oven and, ultimately, to drive sales. I had continued to write a number of commissioned books in my own time and at my own expense on top of my job at the Electricity Council. There was actually some friction around my books. One day the bosses called me in and said the only reason I was being asked to write these books was because I was an employee of the Council. I didn't agree with this at all. From my perspective, my books were helpful to people because of what they contained, and, of course, they were helping to support the use of electricity in the home, which was really my job. I pointed out I was doing all of my writing outside of work time using my own resources and equipment, so I didn't really feel he was justified in having any say over them. Faced with something of an ultimatum I was not willing to accept, I said that I would continue to write, albeit sometimes under my *nom de plume* of Marie Emmerson.

Friction extended to how I was treated as a woman generally. We used to have weekly management meetings, and I of course was the only senior woman in a room full of men. I, along with some of my male colleagues, would smoke during these meetings. The men would pass comment about my smoking, without commenting on the males present who were also lighting up. I remember one particular meeting where someone was having a dig at me for smoking, whereupon I said: "Well at least you can see what my vices are. There is no telling what you get up to behind closed doors." He went as red as a beetroot, so I had clearly touched a nerve, and a Jenny Job was accomplished!

Friction aside, Marks and Spencer negotiated with Octopus Books to be the exclusive UK distributor for the book. And so it was that I ended up writing one of the biggest-selling microwave cookery books of all time: *The Marks and Spencer Book of Microwave Cooking*, which first appeared in 1983. The development process was as arduous as it was rigorous. Anything I have ever written down as a recipe is guaranteed to work, and from my time in laboratory testing I was used to being under very strict and transparent conditions of accountability. Consequently, it made sense for me to carry this over into my recipes. Each recipe was therefore tested fully by me three times.

Electric current in the home fluctuates, and this can actually affect cooking time, so it was vital for me to test out my recipes as vigorously as possible in order to ensure success in the finished printed article. I had to buy all of the ingredients myself, at my own expense. Luckily, however, I was able to use the laboratory appliances to prepare the food as these still needed to be tested for performance and safety, so at least my home kitchen wasn't completely overrun. Furthermore, it wasn't a question of cooking the same dish three times one after the other. I had to let the microwave completely cool and ensure ingredients were straight out of the fridge, to replicate the experience of someone who would just be attempting this for the first time in their own home whilst reading the book. Microwaves, other types of oven and even food containers all retain heat whatever has been cooked in them before, so it was important to space out the three different test versions.

The book was translated into French (*Les Micro-ondes*) — if you can persuade a French housewife then you're doing something right! A million-seller perhaps, but sadly that didn't translate into a million pounds. I was paid a modest one-off fee for my work, and that was that. I was once asked if I ever popped into M&S to spy on book-buyers, but the thought never even occurred to me! But of course, it was always a thrill when I got my first peek at a printed copy of any new book. Mind you, it still surprises me at how prolific I was, whenever I look at my published back catalogue.

11 THE FACE OF THE ELECTRICITY INDUSTRY

I never really realised it at the time, but in my own way I do think now that I was making a difference to the industry, as an expert, as a Home Economist and as a woman in a male-dominated industry. One of the many things I loved about my job was its sheer diversity. I got involved in promoting the industry in so many ways, from radio and television to events and competitions. Decades before *Junior Bake Off* and the like, we started off the concept of competitive cooking for children. All of the 12 Electricity Boards around the UK would hold local electric cooking competitions for children. These junior chefs would cook for a personality or celebrity, and then there would be a regional winner from each area. The final cook-off would be in London, at the Ritz. Each child would cook for a personality, and the personalities were then invited to the Ritz for tea. It was sometimes televised, or appeared on the news.

British Gas already had a stranglehold on a national *Dial-a-Cook* service in 1982, when the Electricity Council decided to launch *Call-a-Cook* in conjunction with the London Electricity Board. Telephone callers were greeted by part of the *Cook Electric* advertising jingle, *"and the friendly voice of Jenny Webb who will describe the week's recipe and give a preview of the next one in line."* The recipes included such regional delicacies as duck paprika, Eccles cakes and Boodles Orange Fool, but we kicked it off with Welsh honey lamb. Each menu featured a main course and a sweet. *"Be ahead of your neighbours!"* we trumpeted to 1980s cooks. After a hiccup with a well-known fizzy drinks firm querying our *Call-a-Cook* logo, early results were encouraging. Over 1000 calls were coming in each week, so the trial was extended. Recipes were later compiled into a free booklet made available via electricity showrooms.

It was Jenny to the rescue again in 1983, when *Woman* magazine drafted me in to help take the panic out of Christmas by taking phone calls direct from readers on two consecutive days just before the big day. Between 8.30am and 5pm, I was dialled up for advice on planning, buying, cooking and feasting. I do hope I managed to spread some festive calm!

Since the Leatherhead laboratory days, I had become involved in a whole range of regional and national presentations and exhibitions promoting the use of electrical appliances in the home, including one for SEEBOARD in Croydon back in 1977, where locals were invited to come and hear all about microwave cookery with Jenny Webb, *Authoress*!

For exhibitions, I would brief our staff in advance so they would have the right information and knowledge to help customers and make sales. The Ideal Home Exhibition was so much fun and always garnered lots of column inches in the trade and regular press. A little "refreshment" on our stand was always welcomed by reporters. I would rope in friends (and even friends' parents!) to hand out flyers to drum up trade.

The highlight of the events year was Belex, an annual, high-profile conference put on by the electrical industry to attract the attention and of the trade press and media, up until the Electricity Boards were privatised.

Hosting the MEB's Cook Electric Show, early 1980s

This was all about educating and entertaining the press, getting positive coverage for the industry and, of course, building business. It was often focused around getting coverage for women's magazine supplements around electricity in the home and domestic appliances. The gas industry used to attempt something similar, although their offer was centred mainly around cooking and heating, whereas the electricity industry was as broad as it was long in its sheer range and diversity – and it was growing. The vast majority of women used to cook in those days, so if you could get them to use electricity over gas, you were on to a winner. This is what Belex was all about. We also used it to promote new advances in technology. At the final ever Belex in 1988 for example, we first introduced the world to the wonders of the halogen hob. You can actually catch me doing this on my YouTube channel! It was my role to talk about cooking appliances, whilst a male colleague would present other types of appliances like air conditioners and heaters. I would make sure I would do my homework: I had been talking to manufacturers throughout the year so I always had a steady supply of contacts and plenty of news and titbits to create a buzz – embargoed until the day of the presentation of course. I had taken this approach into my daily life when we had all the gas appliances removed from our house. There was no way I could stand up in front of the trade press and extol the virtues of electricity whilst heating my home with gas. I had more than one call from industry journalists, sheepishly apologising for having gas central heating installed in their homes.

There was another major annual exhibition, Naidex, which was tailored to the needs of disabled people and supporting independent living. This included things like controls and knobs which had been adapted for people with limited use of hands, Braille signage, etc. One year I persuaded a washing machine manufacturer to offer us one of their products as a competition prize. Diana Moran – BBC Breakfast's Green Goddess – kindly turned up in her famous green leotard to award it to the lucky winner.

I have often been asked what the rivalry between the electricity and gas industries was like. Food writer Marguerite Patten CBE wrote over 170 cookery books in her lifetime and was one of the first TV cooks. No surprise then that the Electricity Council employed her to help promote the value of electrical power. She had long worked with regional boards, advocating the use of refrigeration and advising on how to prepare cold food. Her recipe books included *Electric Mixers and Blenders* and the wonderfully-titled *How to Cook Perfectly with Electricity*.

Demonstrating a halogen hob to the Queen Mother and Viscountess Rothermere at the Ideal Home Exhibition, 1980s

Fanny Cradock, on the other hand, was snapped up early on by the Gas Council, which had been born from the nationalisation of numerous gas companies. Her gas cookery demonstrations with husband Johnnie propelled her to enormous, and enduring, fame. Sadly I never met Fanny, but I did manage to catch a number of her stage shows. She was tremendously entertaining thanks to her remarkable ability to hold the rapt attention of large audiences as she whisked and prepared food, whilst hectoring her long-suffering old man. Fanny was also famously scathing of her first microwave oven, with her and Johnnie approaching it "with the trepidation of two people returning to a reactor station after a leak".

Marguerite, meanwhile, became a good friend to me. In the early 1980s, she approached me with the unique idea of us writing a book together. She would write and test the recipes for conventional cooking and I would do the same for microwave ovens. Back then, Marguerite was still very new to using this type of energy. We each thoroughly tested every recipe of course, aiming to give the reader two sets of instructions so that they could compare the relative merits for themselves. By awarding a star rating, we offered our own forthright recommendations at-a-glance for the best method. With beautiful colour illustrations, we packed in all sorts of handy tips too, from the basics of cheese on toast to speedy fruit jams. The book's working title was *The Unconventional Cookbook* but it was finally published in 1984 as *Two-Way Cookbook*. The first print run sold over 100,000 copies, sparking a reprint in 1985. What better validation for Marguerite's idea?

I made numerous radio and television appearances, and this was a part of the job that I loved. Typically, I would be asked to talk about a particular aspect of electricity, and this would often fall into two camps: energy efficiency and saving money, and – when the media went to town on microwaves – the all-important (and often misreported) safety aspect.

The fact of the matter is that there was never a particular safety issue with microwave ovens. As with all other appliances, electrical safety also applied to microwaves, however the media are never ones to let the truth get in the way of a good story, particularly when there are column inches to be filled and money to be made on the back of them.

Electricity Council press shot, early 1980s

My retro YouTube channel now holds a number of TV appearances I made in the 1980s and 90s, presenting and discussing a range of various household electrical appliances, cookery trends and more, but my on-air spots began with radio back in the 1970s. I was quite a regular at BBC

Broadcasting House in London, chatting to the likes of Jimmy Young on Radio 2, Brian Redhead on Radio 4, and Jimmy Mack on BBC Radio Scotland. I was called on to offer advice on cookery, appliances and how to save energy on local radio, too.

Radio 4 asked me to peer in my crystal ball in January 1977 for a series called *Living in the 80s*. Back then the silicon chip was sparking a revolution in the electronics industry. Reporter George Luce asked me to speculate on where it might take us. Alas no audio survives, just a cutting from the dear old *Radio Times*, so goodness knows how many of my predictions came true in the decade that followed. In the late 1970s, I would sometimes join Norman Tozer on Radio 4 for a quirky five-minute show on Saturdays at 7.55am called *It's a Bargain*. Sadly, I have no recordings of these early appearances. But happily, thanks to the Tellex Broadcasting Reporting Service, which provided transcripts to companies back then, I know exactly what I had to say on 24th September 1977 about the differences between microwave and conventional cooking. As new ovens weren't widely available, Norman was only able to give a BBC guide price on two microwave models: the Toshiba ER556 at £189 and the Moffat 4000 at £220.50 – close to £1400 in today's money. A few years had to elapse before prices dropped to encourage wider take-up.

I even appeared on Radio 3 in the same year for a series called *Lifelines – Home and Family* which offered practical advice for anyone running or setting up a home. Presenter Irene Wyndham wanted to know which appliances really cut down on housework, how to choose labour-saving devices and how to know which household gadgets were safe to use. I, of course, duly obliged. I got to know Sue Cook quite well, after several spots on Radio 4's consumer show *You and Yours,* discussing home matters and budgeting. I was also called on to fight the corner for the electrical industry including in response to the spate of media scares over using microwave ovens. In August 1978 I was required to offer reassurances to Sue following sensational and outlandish health claims made by ITV's *World in Action* based on reports from America.

The year 1989 was another challenging one as alarm bells rang once more, prompting the government to order a detailed study of microwave ovens. By this time, over 50% of the population owned one, so it was my job to help counter fears over food not reaching sufficient temperatures to kill bacteria. Derek Jameson invited me on to his Radio 2 breakfast show in April 1990, allowing me to advise users of the correct way to use their appliances to ensure food was always piping hot. It all seems terribly quaint now, but we concluded our interview – which you can hear in all its glory on my YouTube channel – by giving an address for listeners to write to for a fact sheet, making sure they included a stamped, addressed envelope. No emails or texts in 1990, let alone social media! Calling his studio *The Bunker,* it was all part of Derek's charm to call me and his other female guests "*My dear*" on air.

But it was an altogether different experience when I arrived to speak to Brian Redhead on BBC Radio 4's morning news flagship *Today.* Of course, this was way before online listening via apps or streaming services. So any live interview on a major national radio network to discuss a news story had terrific impact. Quotes were often picked up by newspaper journalists for their lunchtime editions. I was pretty familiar with microphones by this point in my career, and with what the presenters expected from me. This came in particularly handy while discussing the costs of keeping warm in winter, with the electricity industry firmly in the firing line.

When I arrived at the BBC's HQ to talk to Brian, I politely turned down the offer of some breakfast in the Green Room. I quietly waited until being ushered into the studio, and with a finger to his lips, the producer warned me not to speak while the red on-air light was shining. I was convinced they were expecting me to be a complete broadcasting novice. Brian instantly went for the jugular. Many Britons were struggling to balance family budgets and pay their electricity bills, he complained. There had been a particularly spiky caller who was deeply upset at the cost of her fuel bills, stating that she had resorted to wearing a woolly hat at home to keep warm. I found myself in the somewhat unlikely position of agreeing with her 100 per cent, saying that the majority of body heat is lost through the head and that consequently wearing a hat was a very sensible thing to do under the circumstances! Not that the listeners would have known, but my host looked pretty crestfallen when I congratulated her. I don't know whether the caller was impressed with my advice, but it certainly seemed to hit the right notes back at the office. My phone rang all morning with congratulatory calls from senior managers. And it was heartening when the Chairman, Sir Austin Wyeth Bunch, dropped me a note. *"If only we could get this understanding across of how much the industry cares in the way you so obviously depict, we would be better off altogether."* Another Jenny Job pulled off.

Local radio, too, was always hungry for material. Back in the 1970s and 80s, way before down-the-line interview spots were created, the Electricity Council had joined the trend to promote new campaigns with syndicated interviews sent out on reel-to-reel tapes. These arrived ready to use with an accompanying cue sheet for the presenter. Doesn't it sound pre-historic these days? So, I taped all sorts of staged interviews at our HQ which were then sent out and played all over the country to bolster local programmes. These certainly helped to get our industry message across.

Even after I left the industry, I was still invited to appear on various radio shows to share my knowledge. In 1996, I had great fun in the six-week run-up to Christmas when I was invited to become a seasonal consultant for Bibi Baskin on Talk Radio. This was a new national phone-in station launched the year before on medium wave. Bibi was very well known in Ireland thanks to her own RTÉ chat show, and she had crossed the sea for a number of new projects in the UK. Holed up in a studio for three hours each week alongside our fellow jovial expert Mike London, we got to know each other pretty well, fielding calls from listeners on all manner of queries. I shared everything from money-saving tips to festive recipe hints and tastings. I am a great believer in cooking in advance as much as possible and freezing it ready for the big day. All of this culminated in me and Bibi spending the afternoon on air together on Christmas Day. I, of course, arrived in my very best festive frock and high heels, so Bibi was greatly amused when I produced a pair of fluffy pink slippers to wear in the studio! Well, a lady likes her comforts.

It was terrific to be asked in 1998 to help celebrate the hundredth anniversary of the Fairy brand name first appearing. on a revolutionary bar of soap made from olive oil. Manufacturers Procter & Gamble had a lot to celebrate, as over 13 million UK households were by then buying 150 million bottles of Fairy washing up liquid each year, 57% of the total market. So I was booked to spend a day talking down the line to local and regional stations all over the country. The average family wash in 1898 took three days to complete. Even in the 1950s, women were spending around 75 hours per week on household chores. So did that mean we were all now living in dirty hovels? Cue Jenny to talk about the wonders of labour-saving devices – and the products made to aid maximum efficiency. Boiling clothes and rubbing Fairy green soap on collars and cuffs started to be replaced by the arrival in the UK in the 1950s of washing machines. This prompted the launch of Fairy Snow washing powder. For washing dishes, people traditionally used powders or crystals, which made them very slippery and caused breakages. But after much testing, green Fairy liquid had arrived in the 1960s. I knew my subject off by heart, after spending a day repeating all this information over and over to each presenter. And when they each brought up celebrities who appeared in those famous TV ads, I was able to tell them that Rochdale-born film star and singer, Gracie Fields, first advertised Fairy on Radio Luxembourg in 1937.

Like radio, my television appearances were varied. These days media training is quite the thing, but there was no such luxury for me when I nervously stepped in front of the camera for the first time. As to what to wear, the only thing I had heard was that blue was not a good colour on screen. I did get apprehensive of course, so it was all the more important to be fully across the subject for discussion. One of my very early TV appearances was on the BBC's Asian magazine *Gharbar* in 1981, which revolved around tips for saving energy and keeping down bills in what was still a nationalised, publicly-run industry. As the 1980s progressed and use of electrical appliances in the home became widespread, I would often be asked to compare different types of appliances and their relative merits. In 1984, I recorded a series of breakfast TV features for TV-AM's *Check Out* presented by Lynn Faulds Wood. These included microwaves, food mixers and dishwashers. After writing a couple of microwave cookery books to accompany Yorkshire Television's popular *Farmhouse Kitchen*, the producers even had a chat with me over the possibility of a presenting role, but this didn't come to fruition. Aberdeen was my next destination in 1985 for Grampian TV's *Pennywise* to talk yet again about the wonders of microwave cookery. The hosts Muriel Clark and Anne Brand were great fun to work with. It's a widely-held view that this money-saving series inspired Victoria Wood's canny spoof *McConomy* on her BBC TV comedy series *Victoria Wood As Seen On TV*.

Appearances continued into the 90s, including on the BBC's daytime discussion show *Esther* (hosted by Esther Rantzen) highlighting the importance of thorough domestic cleaning, BBC2's *All Mod Cons* covering the history of electrical appliances in the home and an interview with best-selling *Bridget Jones* author Helen Fielding for the BBC documentary series on the history of home entertaining, *A Slice of Life*.

My most recent TV appearance was on a different subject entirely, and completely unplanned. Around Richmond, being under the flightpath for Heathrow Airport, it was not entirely unheard of for desperate stowaways to fall from an aeroplane as it lowered its undercarriage. It was mid-June 2015, and a body had been discovered on the roof of the notonthehighstreet.com building near Richmond station. It had been confirmed that it had fallen from a plane. The next day, as I walked through Richmond, I was approached by a BBC TV reporter and asked to give a very brief interview as to my reaction to the tragic news, and told it would be aired later that day. Although I had not mentioned it to anyone nor had I seen it, several friends did, and left me telephone messages. However, the one from my friend in Canada was the best. As an avid BBC viewer she was listening to the BBC News in her kitchen, recognised my voice, and turned to see me on the screen. We later laughed and agreed that, typical of me and not even seeking it out, a microphone and camera had found me.

I had also been busy putting out consumer content in a variety of other media throughout this time. The 1980s had seen a concerted effort to try to better meet the needs of electricity consumers with disabilities. I recorded a number of guides and brochures which were made available on audio cassette tapes. And once again by the wonder of technology, I was able to record *Jenny Webb's Top 20 Recipes for the Talking Microwave*. I was also delighted to host a recipe spot for a weekly talking magazine tape sent out to listeners across the UK with a visual impairment. *Weekend Listener* was a lively hour presented by Peter Reed, who became a great friend. Emma Forbes did a beauty spot, while a host of big names gave up their time for star interviews each week. One Christmas, the team all got together to record a comic murder mystery in a country house, introduced by EastEnders actress Anita Dobson. I can't think why they thought of me when I was cast to play the cockney downstairs cook, Mrs Scrunge!

Weekend Listener tapes were supplied free of charge every week by the charity, Sound Press for the Blind – quite a ground-breaking approach for the time. The content was varied and similar to that found in a newspaper's Sunday supplement. For several years I was a weekly contributor covering not just electrical information but giving commentaries on other subjects. One month I was asked to do an interview at a French training centre for new guide dog users. The centre included a large outside area and was constructed to include the many hazards a blind person would encounter. These included stairs, bridges, traffic lights, various road surfaces and obstacles such as roadworks. I was asked if I would care to be blindfolded and, with a guide dog, to walk the course whilst recording a commentary at the same time. Before this, I was given the opportunity to observe a volunteer and his dog walking the route. Afterwards, we had lunch with the management and the volunteer was seated next to me with his dog lying between us. The lunch was delicious and the conversation stimulating. However, I became aware of my thigh being stroked. I had a quandary as to whether to say something or to let it go. My decision was made as it was not something I would tolerate with a sighted person. Thus, I said: "I'm sorry, that's my leg you are stroking, not your dog." The hand was swiftly removed.

Whilst we were there, we drove to a region where the local delicacy was lambs' testicles. As usual, my job was to eat some and comment on the experience. We found the restaurant for lunch and the others selected their food and I had the speciality. When served, the presentation of mine was similar to the other dishes and if I had not known I would not have been able to identify the food. It was really nice, tender, rather like chicken and served in a sauce. To complete my description I asked to see some uncooked samples for accuracy. They arrived presented on a silver platter. The men with me had a very interesting reaction!

My travelling exploits around that period weren't purely for business. Living where I did, we would see Concorde passing over our house daily as it flew in to land. In contrast, my mother told me that when she was a child an aeroplane pilot would follow the railway tracks to navigate a journey, and she recalled chasing the plane as it was at low level and relatively slow.

To travel by Concorde was beyond the price of ordinary people and so we could only dream. However, at that time there was a company promoting this flying experience to the masses. Their "inexpensive" flights were just for a one-way experience, and not to Europe, the Far East or the USA, but to Heathrow Airport from Stansted Airport - a total of 40 minutes!

My mother was in her seventies and I felt she would love to be able to compare her childhood scamper to the fastest passenger plane that ever existed. I also invited my mother-in-law so she, too, could share the experience. We joined a coach with others which drove us to Stansted and waited in the lounge to be called to board for Concorde flight BA908. On board, we were greeted with courtesy as if we were VIPs, served champagne, and throughout the flight the Captain and crew gave a fascinating commentary. We received a certificate and an information pack. My mother wanted more and even took a sick bag as a further souvenir.

On our return home we sat in our garden and waved to a Concorde as it brought back passengers from somewhere else in the world. A brief flight which will nevertheless always be a wonderful memory.

Celebrating Christmas with Bibi Baskin, the year we worked together on Talk Radio

12 BY ROYAL REQUEST

En route to Buckingham Palace

On the morning of Saturday, 9 March 1991, an ordinary buff envelope, marked *On Her Majesty's Service*, arrived. Little could I have known that I would find within the invitation of a lifetime. It was from the Ministry of Agriculture,

Fisheries and Food and read:

Dear Mrs Webb

Her Majesty the Queen will give garden parties at Buckingham Palace this year on 9, 11 and 18 July, and Sir Derek Andrews, as permanent Secretary of the Ministry of Agriculture, Fisheries and Food, has been asked by the Lord Chamberlain's Office to make a limited number of nominations for the honour of invitation. Sir Derek would like to send forward your name and I should be grateful if you would let me know by 13 March whether you would be able to accept an invitation.

I could hardly believe what I was reading and so I read it several times to be sure that I had not misunderstood the contents. It was amazing. How could anyone not wish to be invited?

The following Monday I telephoned and confirmed that I was delighted to accept and, being me, I would be free on any date they desired! I read also that there was no guarantee of an invitation, but even with this well in mind, the following week I went out to buy a new outfit. The long wait was on and it was not until mid-June that I received a gold-edged invitation from Her Majesty Queen Elizabeth II inviting me to attend. I had declined on Brian's part as his heart condition would not enable him to stand or walk for long distances or periods. Leading up to July, he was also complaining of chest pains so I was concerned that I might not be able to attend at all.

The day arrived after a restless and excited night. What a day for a garden party: the skies were grey and heavy with pouring rain. The rain continued until lunchtime then the clouds broke up and slowly but surely the sun shone through. I changed into my specially-bought ensemble and, with much excitement, the girls in the office crowded around, took photos and enjoyed the anticipation of the event. Even the men seemed interested. I wore a large, brimmed, smooth straw hat and a dress of yellow-and-white flowers, a waist jacket in poppy red with gold buttons and a cravat attached to the jacket of the dress material. The accessories were black.

The majority of men were in grey morning suits with top hats whilst the women were dressed in all manner of elegant dresses and hats. The colours were vibrant yellows, oranges, greens, blues, reds and every variation and pattern of colour and fabric. It was all very orderly and although nobody was giving orders, the guests were politely guided to the gates of the palace. We steadily moved forward towards the policeman, clutching our blue guest tickets. He glanced at each and then we crunched across the courtyard towards the arch. A breeze caught the skirts of women and they gently wafted around their legs. For those of us with brimmed hats we had to hold them in place to avoid them being whipped off our heads. We passed the red-jacketed and Busby-topped guard and entered through into the inner courtyard.

All four sides of the palace had windows, and at ground level enormous columns supported the structure giving shelter to those who would walk beneath. Opposite was the glass-fronted canopy so often seen on the television when the royal family enter their cars and coaches. Masters at Arms in their morning suits guided the two snakes of people to various entrances. I was fortunate and entered the one used by the royal family. There was a murmur of guests' voices as we continued to move forward onto the red carpet and up the stairs. Footmen took our guest tickets and we walked into the hall.

The hall was very large with thick carpeting on the floor, around which were settees in rich brocade, and chairs with red plush seats and backs surrounded by golden painted wood. Some had what looked to be GR or ER embossed on the chair back supports. To the front and right, steps went up to a gallery. To the right of one set of steps an enormous fireplace fitting enclosed a clock face and, to the left, an entrance to another part of the palace could be seen. Along the gallery immediately in front were large portraits of women beautifully painted and framed in gold. They seemed to be of royal wives.

The ceiling was quite low being white panels surrounded by square frames of golden carved wood. Through open doors we passed into a room with a semi-circle of windows and a door leading to the terrace. Here again, there were beautifully upholstered settees and chairs and in each corner a lick of deep blue and gold china in a display cabinet. I descended the steps onto a gravel path and joined groups of people on the lawn. Looking at the top of the building I noticed security men with binoculars and other devices. They were silhouetted against the sky and there to be seen throughout the afternoon. Meanwhile, the Beefeaters were standing in order whilst the Master at Arms mingled with guests selecting those who would be presented. At 4pm the band struck up the anthem, and standing at the tip of the terrace steps were the Queen and Prince Philip. They moved down the steps and were followed by the Queen Mother, Princess Alexandra and Angus Ogilvy. Princess Alexandra moved along the lawn between lines of people and stopped about three feet away from me to speak with a couple in front.
From here I decided to enjoy the garden, and walk the

perimeter. To the side of the palace I took the path. First I enjoyed the herbaceous borders full of flowers such as sweet peas, foxgloves and hollyhocks, then the rose garden with roses in full bloom and a small temple-like construction in which one could sit and take in the view. To my left the lawns rose and fell with trees and bushes giving shade, and in the central area was the famous lake.

Continuing my walk I saw the tennis courts and then came upon a rockery. By now, my feet and body needed a rest, thus I chose to sit on a rock which faced the lake and pondered, enjoying the scene. In the background was the continuous throb and hum of London traffic and the strains of music from the band. After about 20 minutes I was joined by another woman from Newcastle. She too was unescorted. We sat for a while then continued our walk to take tea on the lawn. The tea area took the form of a long open-fronted marquee. Inside a counter covered the entire length, and this was groaning with tiny sandwiches, drop scones, cakes, tartelettes and other teatime favourites. None seemed larger than three inches in diameter. China and silver were stacked and sparkling whilst the black-and-white-uniformed waitresses dispensed tea, iced coffee, lemon drinks and shallow tubs of ice cream served on a plate with a teaspoon. Along the front of the marquee was a slender shelf on which the guests politely jostled to place their cups. A number of chairs and small tables were strategically placed nearby, but these were taken for most of the afternoon.

I walked back to the palace with my newfound acquaintance and said goodbye as she was to take an early train back to Newcastle. I then walked to the side of the palace and sat upon a garden seat surrounding the enormous trunk of an old tree. The tree must have been several hundred years old as the foliage was like some great umbrella. It was about 5.30pm so I sat and studied my fellow guests. They were all beginning to droop. Hats were being held, gloves were stuffed into hand bags and faces wore the look of aching feet. The breeze had picked up, and many of those still wearing hats had lost the fight to keep them on. Frequently, the breeze tossed them off their heads then tumbled them along the lawn, sharply followed by the gallant gentlemen retrievers.

Three Rolls Royces were parked nearby and by now those who had lost their inhibitions and awe were wandering around them and daring to peak through the windows. Alas, my rest was not for long. A Master at Arms came towards the seat, and asked that everyone move, as the royal family would be returning to the palace across the lawn. A throng of several people deep lined the thoroughfare for the royals. Then Beefeaters with their leader marched smartly through the centre and, two-by-two, stood in wait. Not long after, the royal party came through and, unlike their guests, looked as fresh as they had at the very beginning.

It was now 5.55pm, and the party was over. Guests started to squash up the terrace steps to return through the palace. Meanwhile, notices had been put out on either side of the steps indicating that guests could use a side door. I smiled and decided this was for me as I walked to the side of the palace to exit. By none other than the Electricians' Entrance!

13 THE END OF AN ERA

I think the media found me very useful - and accessible. Perhaps that's why I was good at my job. I feel that I had a good, long and successful career, starting with the Electricity Board in the 1950s, the General Electric Company and then the Electricity Council, including at its Appliance Testing Laboratories. This was now a time of great change in the electrical industry. With privatisation, the role of the Electricity Council had altered, reflecting a shift in the landscape that went all the way from how the industry was structured to how electricity was provided to the home and the purposes for which it was used. The Electricity Council ceased to exist, and the Electricity Association was born. The Association's job was to respond to the newly-privatised model and make it a success. Still based in Millbank Tower, and still working to promote the industry, electricity was fast becoming like oxygen – something that was absolutely vital for everyday life. Zola had been right.

Some important work remained to be carried out in the domain of microwave ovens, however. In 1990, the Ministry of Agriculture, Fisheries and Food set up a working group committee of experts including manufacturers and retailers to investigate the use and possible inconsistent labelling of microwave ovens. I was invited to represent both the Microwave Association and the electricity supply industry. I had a lot of experience and knowledge from the early days of the introduction of microwave ovens to the UK public, as Head of Performance Testing at Electricity Council and of the Appliance Testing Laboratory. I had written and published many books and articles, lectured students and trainees and advised the media with regard to the use and safety of microwaves, and was Chairman of the Microwave Association. Initially, MAFF chaired the group but by the end of 1992 I was invited to take the Chair, and government representatives sat as members.

At the end of 1992, the government published a 12-page booklet, *Food Sense – The New Microwave Labels* giving information as to the production of a label on all microwave ovens and listing all the oven models and manufacturers on sale in the UK. In 1993, the comprehensive final publication was launched under Crown Copyright, confirming all the details of the scheme including label design, instructions for the testing of the labelling, and other relevant information.

And yet, the landscape was changing fast. Post-privatisation, the newly-formed Electricity Association ended up taking quite a lot of the flak for changes brought about in the industry and how they impacted consumers, particularly if said consumers were left feeling worse off than before. The need to actively promote electricity, however, was becoming less and less apparent with each year that passed, and with it, my role took on a reduced relevance. They eventually called me Communications Manager, but in reality I was now managing little but myself. It was at this precise point that I realised I had essentially become redundant. My work was no longer necessary, as electricity usage was now completely widespread. Added to which, the industry no longer wanted to provide the outreach and communications service it had previously taken such pride in. The companies were simply there to make money.

One of my later press shots for the Electricity Association

I had changed bosses a few times and by now had a great line manager. I still had my own office overlooking the Thames. I loved my job and I enjoyed working with the media, and especially working with *people*. Things were still rosy enough, but I could start to sense some resistance to what I was doing, and to my specific role. I had been working on a monthly home economics bulletin which was to be sent out to the entire industry, but this kept being delayed internally and sent back to me. I felt that there was a move to get rid of me, but I dug my heels in and ignored it, not wanting to give anyone the satisfaction of a reaction. Sure enough, I was eventually offered a redundancy, the terms of which I rejected after consulting a financial advisor. It was promptly upped, and I accepted. I had effectively been forced out after all those years, but the entire industry was virtually unrecognisable from when I started, and I had given it a long run.

I retired in 1994. It was also a year of huge personal upheaval, as it was then that Brian, my husband of 34 years, died after a protracted illness which had lasted more than a decade. He was still only in his 50s. What should have been the beginning of a new era of relaxation and happiness together was marred by this shattering, devastating event, and I prioritised looking after myself for once, to get through what was a highly traumatic period.

14 SATURDAY, 29 OCTOBER 1994

Dinner

Home-made Pea Soup

Chicken in Wine Sauce
Puréed Carrot and Suede
Cauliflower in Sauce
Mangetout
New Potatoes

Brandy Trifle
Cheese and Grapes

15 AN OLD LADY AND HER SUITCASE

My first priority after retirement, and in the wake of Brian's tragically early death, was to do precisely nothing, and this I did for a year. I had lost my husband and my job, and for once it was time to relax. I then did some small bits of private PR work for the industry, but I had essentially finished my working life. Having generated many documents and files regarding the development and use of domestic electrical appliances over the years, I was extremely keen to ensure that these wouldn't be lost now that I was no longer working. So I sent a load of them to the terrific Science and Industry Museum in Manchester. Visitors can still ask to search all these files under my name, as well as the Electricity Council and Association.

I got my Labrador, Sophie, just after Brian died. Whilst not a like-for-like replacement, she was at least warm-blooded, and an adorable black fur baby. It was my friend Frank who had suggested the name Sophie, but I liked it and it stuck. It also suited her. The early days with Sophie weren't the easiest. On one occasion I woke up to find she had come into my room while I was asleep and proceeded to destroy everything in it. I had slept through the whole affair. She was a happy, loving dog and I had her for 12 wonderful years. She was a surrogate for Brian in more ways than one: she even used to sleep on his pillow. Sophie was quite the tart actually. I gradually started entertaining again, and she became a fixture at my many dinner parties. She would corner whomever happened to be enjoying a handful of Bombay Mix – a favourite pre-dinner appetiser of mine at the time – and gaze imploringly at the poor, unsuspecting guest until they had no choice but to hand over their snack. It's fair to say she became quite a well-proportioned lady in her later years.

Entertaining friends at home, 1995

I had always loved seeing the world, and I now found myself with a wanderlust that I hadn't been able to fulfil while I had been working and during the years of Brian's illness. I decided I had to get out there and travel again. So that is exactly what I did, becoming an old lady and her suitcase, occasionally for work, but increasingly – and soon exclusively – for pleasure!

South Africa, 1996

Whilst on business in South Africa, I took the opportunity to enjoy a few extra days to go sightseeing. My base was near Johannesburg, where I discovered an amusement park called Gold Reef City, which was built on the site of a gold mine which dated from 1890 but which had closed in 1971.

However, it was possible to visit both the mine and its museum, which was good enough for me as I was not interested in the attraction of the amusements, rides, restaurant or casino.

The mine site looked as if it had been left on the day it closed, and even the shaft cage looked genuine, although it was possibly a replica. Regardless, it still appeared to have a realistic atmosphere. Before entering the cage we had to don a hard hat, whilst some had handheld torches. Our guide was called Tom and had worked in the mine for 38 years until his retirement. The shaft was over 700 feet deep, but we visitors could only go so far. On entering the cage it felt very rickety and, as the gates clanged shut and the cage lumbered downwards, I must confess I felt rather apprehensive.

On arrival, the electric lighting was dim but we were reminded that the miners had no such luxury, having had to work long hours by candlelight, and our feelings of being hot and claustrophobic were nothing in comparison to their conditions. The tour continued along a tunnel where we saw gold reef deposits and a demonstration by candlelight as to how they bored holes in the rock. After such a small taste of being underground, it was more than enough of an experience to understand the terrible conditions in which people had worked, and a great relief to return to the fresh air on the surface.

Later in the museum, a demonstration was given illustrating fake gold being melted in a grey metal crucible and placed into a raging furnace where the heat was so intense that it turned the crucible into a vivid glowing orange. Once removed from the furnace, the molten "gold" was poured into 55Ib ingot moulds. There was also more to see but the highlight for me was to touch a real gold ingot valued at $750,000. If only I could have taken it home as a souvenir.

USA, 1997

I was on a coach tour along the west coast of the USA, which included a two-day visit to Las Vegas. On arrival at our hotel I was aware of the constant clank of the handles and the ringing bells of the fruit machines whilst the seated gamblers concentrated on the whirling fruits on their screens. The vast area was full of people wandering, looking or sitting at the various gaming tables where the noise of clattering wheels, cards being turned and the croupiers' voices were all part of the atmosphere.

A highlight was to visit the 5-6 million year-old Grand Canyon with a choice of travelling by coach or by a small light aircraft. I chose to fly one way and meet up with the coach and the other passengers to return to the hotel. This meant that my time traversing the Canyon would be shortened and limited but on the up side, I would actually fly over the huge gorge, and view more of the famous sights from the air.

By this time we, as passengers, were very friendly and outgoing with each other, and we had an excellent guide. The guide asked if I would be willing to act as the leader for the few of us who would fly whilst she escorted the majority by coach. I accepted and the flying group agreed and one even gave me a flat bright yellow-and-white striped cap to indicate my forthcoming position of responsibility.

As the coach passengers would be leaving much earlier, I was briefed on my role and given the appropriate documentation for the next day. Over dinner I explained to the flying group, and (with tongue in cheek) I warned them that if they were not at our arranged meeting place, I would leave them behind as the planes would be waiting for us at the specified time.

I may have seemed relaxed, but I began to realise what a responsibility I had taken on and so I was up much earlier than the others. I had been told that a coach would be outside to take us to the airfield, and thought that this would be an easy start. On exiting the hotel I found the scene to be really hot and jammed with numerous coaches and people. What a beginning, and I was more than concerned as I had a time factor to take into account. There was no way our coach would be able to park immediately outside the hotel so I needed to find ours. With my cap and clipboard, and hoping I appeared to be an experienced guide, I began my search to try to identify where it was, and accosted every coach driver I could find. Finally, hot and exhausted, I met the group and ushered them to our coach.

Our driver was a delightful and handsome African American man with a great sense of humour, and having explained that I was not an official guide, I sat in the front, took the microphone and introduced myself and Willie (the driver). He joined in the fun as I asked him to answer my various questions about himself and the scenery on our route. To my relief, we arrived at the airfield on time, and made our way to a small single-storey building where I handed over our documentation and, as requested, asked the weight of each member of the group. The pilots of each plane then selected who they would have as passengers. At last I could revert to being myself as I sat in one of the five planes.

The trip was fantastic and we eventually landed in the Canyon and joined the others. Our guide asked how we got on and I was rather flattered as they said that I could take over as a guide whenever I wanted! For me, my short experience had been sufficient to illustrate it was not all glamour and that such a job was not an easy one.

China, 1998

Years ago I was first aware of the now famous Terracotta Warriors after visiting Selfridges, who had held an exhibition relating to the discovery of them. It was this that inspired me to know more and see them in situ. However, my trip to China was memorable with an itinerary covering so much more. This was achieved by travelling to various sights by coach, train and air. This enabled me to learn of the history of the numerous dynasties and their influence, visit ancient buildings and experience the culture. As a result, it certainly made me realise that the history of the UK was so very young in comparison.

The site of the Warriors was Xian (pronounced *She Ann*), originally known as Chang'an. However, long before their discovery, it was here that the Chinese were the first to make silk. The wife of the Yellow Emperor was known to have been spinning it back in 2550 BC, but divulging the secret of making it, and the export of silkworms, were capital offences. It was not until 138 BC that the Emperor sent a courtier on a secret mission of discovery. The result was the beginning of the Silk Road.

Only in 1974 did two farmers digging some land find the first artefacts, which they took to an archaeologist. What they had stumbled up upon was the burial kingdom of the

Emperor Ying Zheng, who assumed the title of Shi Haung. He was only 13 years old when he became Emperor but immediately started the construction of his tomb which was designed to secure his immortality. At his instruction it was to cover both material and personal wants and to include palaces, pavilions, jewels, horse-driven chariots and a lake, to name a few. He also needed an army to protect him, and had 8000 life-size warriors made, each unique and with individual features and expressions.

It was thrilling to see what had been excavated to date, but it will take many years before it will all be uncovered. It was a thrilling day but with a tremendous bonus. I met one of the original farmers, had a photograph taken with him and, having purchased a book, asked him to sign it. The day finished with dinner at a famous dumpling restaurant. There was also an area with tanks containing various types of fish, turtles and toads, all of which would be used in the dumplings. At my table we managed to eat 35 each, and all had a different filling. I must confess that I did not ask what was in the fillings, but they were extremely tasty.

A Japanese Boat Ride, 1999

I had the opportunity to take the well-known Hozugawa River Boat Ride from Tanba-Kameoka to Arashiyama, which covered a 16-kilometre stretch of the river and would take two hours. After several days of business, I felt that it would give me a chance to relax and enjoy the trip which would cover different scenery along the route. On arrival at the starting point I was surprised to see that the craft was a low slender sixteen-person flat-bottomed boat without seats, and we would be sitting on the deck.

An interesting start, I thought, especially when we were told that the three male pilots (as they were called) were very experienced, would always have to come from the same village, and had to train for ten years to navigate the route with long bamboo poles instead of oars. Having this explained, we boarded the craft without life jackets and set off, with one pilot at the rear and the other two at the front of the boat. At last it dawned on me that the ride was not a gentle cruise along the river but one which included the river flow, negotiating rapids, avoiding rocks, getting wet and, in-between, looking at the scenery. It was a real adventure - even though not quite what I had expected.

Australia, 2000

Wherever there has been an opportunity to take a balloon ride, I have always been "up" for it! It is so exciting to see the balloon being inflated, transforming itself from a long skinny mass of fabric and rope into a gigantic colourful sphere with a little oblong basket hanging beneath it. Balloons I have taken have always held seven passengers plus the pilot, although some can accommodate any number from two to 30.

Getting into a basket is no mean feat, and some form of help is always needed by way of steps or a push up the rear! Once on board, the pilot lights a propane liquid burner to heat the air in the balloon and it then rises and moves under his control throughout the flight. The silence is unique and only broken by the whoosh of the burner.

Everything was normal on this particular flight until the pilot said that we were to make an emergency landing as soon as possible. As to why, I never discovered, but without any panic he managed to guide the balloon down to land in an area full of grassy mounds. In doing so the basket tipped onto its side. Nobody was hurt and we sort of scrambled out. Our pilot reassured us that a backup vehicle always keeps in touch with the balloon so help was on its way.

Help arrived and as the balloon was deflated it needed to be rolled up so it could be transported on the back of the trailer. We were asked by the pilot to participate. I decided that it really was not quite my style and so was happy to stand aside and to enjoy a cigarette whilst watching the others crawling around. Once the balloon was mounted on the back of a trailer we were driven back to where we had set out for our champagne breakfast and also a certificate on which was printed: *This is to certify that you did today fly high in the sky over Australia on a spectacular balloon flight with Hot Air.* After the words "*Hot Air*", our pilot added a hand written comment: *And under a more-or-less controlled crash.* For me that was the best flight ever.

Another highlight of my Australia trip was to visit Ayers Rock, which had been "discovered" in 1873 by a European and named after the then-South Australian Chief Secretary, Sir Henry Ayers. It was opened in 1983, and in 1985 returned to its Aboriginal owners whereupon in 1993 it was given once again its real name of Uluru.

The six-million-year-old gigantic sandstone rock has been a sacred place for 10,000 years and is some 348 metres high and 9.4 kilometres in circumference. Although with much history attached to it, it is the manner in which the rock changes colour at sunrise and sunset which often is what the tourists want to see. This is due to the iron mineral within the rock having slowly rusted over the centuries so that, as the sun moves across the sky, it causes Uluru to change from bright red through to pastel shades of blue, grey, pink and brown. On the evening of our arrival we were taken to the Rock just before sunset to enjoy the experience. During the wait, champagne and canapes were served and it was explained that if we wanted to take photos, to wait for a minute between shots to ensure that we could get each colour change as it would be difficult for the eye to judge. It was really exciting as the sun started its descent and I kept sipping the champagne, calling each minute and snapping accordingly. On my return to the UK the prints came back and instead of having six, one of each colour change, I had about 20. In my tiddly state, I had got the timing completely wrong!

Earlier in the day on the back of a Harley Davidson motorbike I took about a 50-kilometre round-trip excursion to the Olgas, another famous sacred Aboriginal site with a fantastic series of 36 domed rocks covering an area of about 22 square kilometres. After the excursion was completed we took a drive around the circumference of Uluru. In all honesty, I chose this trip simply to have the experience of riding on such an iconic motorbike, and it was worth every penny.

Determined not to miss another adventure I was up very early the next morning to take a 30-minute helicopter ride to see the effect of the sunrise on Uluru and Olgas before continuing to my next hotspot, Alice Springs. I have had the opportunity to return to Australia since, but am so pleased that I took the excursions at Uluru which, I now know, will never happen again. So the moral of this story is never put off what you can do today.

Finland, 2001

Never having had the chance to go fishing, I was in Finland for a Christmas holiday and it was suggested that I might enjoy ice fishing. Oh yes, I thought so, appropriately clad for the climate, I met my Finnish guide on a selected spot on a frozen lake. He explained that it was essential not to alert any fish, so a hand drill would be used to make a hole in the ice. Then, the fishing line with bait would be lowered down into the hole, and after this it was just a question of waiting until a fish bit. Having been well informed, I started to drill a hole but then asked for the guide to finish it off. Once completed, I lowered my line and waited. And waited. By then I wanted to have a cigarette but as my hands were occupied, and I had had enough, I asked him to take over. At this point I decided that fishing was not for me and went back to the hotel. We returned fishless, and I never went fishing again.

Alternative Transport, India, 2001

The Amber Fort, pronounced Amer, is a deserted city fort and was the Capital of Jaipur State until 1727, when it was transferred to Jaipur. Its construction began in 1592 and continued over numerous years, thus the architecture is both Hindu and Mughal, using both pink and yellow sandstone and white marble. It is sometimes called the Shish Mahal or the Palace of Mirrors as inside it has a huge hall with inlaid panels and mirrored ceilings. It all sounded very interesting and so I decided that it was a sight I had to see, plus as access to it was up a very long steep incline, elephants could be hired as transport to the top.

In a courtyard below the Fort, I encountered six elephants, each with its back covered with brightly-coloured fabric over which was a seat which accommodated four passengers. Behind their heads and sitting astride were the "drivers", all very handsome and resplendent in their traditional dress and large swirling turbans. Mounting the animal was quite a feat as we had to climb some steps onto a platform and then clamber onto the shoulders of the elephant to sit two-by-two and back-to-back. When all the passengers were seated, we set off in a line at a slow lumbering pace along the road towards the Fort. It was a strange experience sitting and moving at such a height with a very large weighty lady leaning heavily on my back and making me feel insecure, so much so that I became more concerned about trying to hold on rather than enjoying the ride. It took about 20 minutes to reach the top but I had to laugh when another elephant must have got bored of the pace and overtook us. The driver told us it was because our elephant was elderly and the younger ones always wanted to go faster. I think that I must have been one of the early tourists as I heard recently that today some 80 elephants are used for making the same journey.

Niagara Falls, 2002

On a holiday overland trip to Eastern Canada and the Rockies, I had the opportunity to visit one of the world's wonders, namely Niagara Falls. In my ignorance, I had not realised it was an area which also included the Niagara Whirlpool, the Mighty Rapids and the Horseshoe Falls (also known as the Canadian Falls) which is the largest in the world, and straddles Canada and the USA, and is hence an international border. My first view was a panoramic one seated in a tour helicopter. From there, I watched enormous amounts of water from the Niagara River tumbling in torrents over the Falls and its spray resembling a mist climbing to the sky, whilst the tour boats looked like tiny blobs in the calmer areas of the waters. The pilot throughout gave a useful commentary as to what we were observing, including the surrounding areas, and confirmed that the Falls were first witnessed by a French explorer in 1698.

On landing, I was awarded a High Flyers Certificate in my name given by the Niagara Helicopters Limited High Flyers Club which confirmed that I had flown on that date over the Falls. Although I was pleased to have it, I had to remember that as a "member" of the club, it did not give me any benefits and they must have given out millions of certificates over numerous years. My next move was to take one of the famous *Maid of the Mist* boats and, unlike the seven-seater helicopter flight, I joined the hundreds of people who were taking the same trip. Each was given a thin blue plastic hooded cape, and like a colony of penguins we shuffled along onto the boat where we stood squashed together like sardines. It was not until recently that it occurred to me that nobody was given any form of life jacket, so I suppose the boat company thought if needed, our capes would keep us afloat!

Having seen the size of the boats from the sky I was a little frightened as we sailed closer to the Falls, especially when I became even more aware of how enormous they were. Added to this, was the tremendous roar of the cascading water and the constant fine spray over everybody which was unbelievable and unnerving. Finally the boat moved into calmer waters and in a very damp state we disembarked. What a day of special memories including the ruination of my makeup after my boat trip when the mist had got onto my face.

Greenland, 2006

As always, any country holds a fascination for me, so a cruise to Greenland, where Nuuk the capital is claimed to be the smallest capital city in the world, was hard to resist. However, when I read that I could take an excursion on a helicopter over the glaciers, I was sold. The helicopter was to land on one of the glaciers and we would then enjoy a glass of whisky served with a piece of 1000 year-old ice! The weather was perfect and seeing the glaciers, snow and icebergs from such a height was magical, but I was surprised to see so much snow having a grey film rather than white. During the flight, the pilot gave a commentary about the history of the glaciers and how the weight of snow and ice pushes the front mass into the sea so that ice flows are formed. Eventually, he landed the helicopter in a very small gap on a glacier then left holding a small ice pick used to chip the ice. On his return, I had my whisky which was enhanced with the ice. On reflection, I wondered if it really was 1000 years old - but it was a trip worth taking. And the whisky was delicious.

Togo, 2009

A coach took my group through Loam, the capital, on well-made roads paved with modern hotels. Eventually we left the city behind to enter by an unmade track into a dense jungle. Here we had to get off at the edge of the village land and stand under an ancient mahogany tree where we were met by the Head Man, who was a very tall, serious and handsome individual dressed in traditional attire. He greeted us in his native language and spoke to the gods to tell them we were welcome. This initiation ensured that we would be saved from any grief during our visit.

Returning to the coach we arrived outside of Sanguera where the Head Man was waiting for us. However, we could not enter but had to stand behind a demarcation line. Presently, the Chief of the village arrived with his entourage. He then followed a spoken ritual using water, and finally a witch doctor appeared and threw himself to the ground. At last we were directed to a clearing in the village where we sat on benches to observe many bare-chested witch doctors in their grass skirts who seemed to be in an hypnotic state, jumping, running and swirling to the singing and clapping of the women in the background.

One held a live chicken high above his head before enclosing it in an earthenware pot and proceeded to bury it in a hole which was then filled with sand and left for four hours. Later, the chicken was taken from the pot and was still alive! Elsewhere, a fire was lit and some of the witch doctors kept putting their hands into the flames and bathing their arms and torsos in it. One was using a knife to cut his body but no cut was apparent. Suddenly, another doctor's grass skirt was alight and as he was in a highly charged state, he swirled at an even higher speed than previously. This was only for a few moments as the others soon put the flames out with their hands. Somehow, I do not think that this was a part of the ceremony.

New Zealand, 2009

I took a trip to the settlement of Paparoa to enjoy the spectacle of the traditional greeting given to family friends and visitors. Before we could enter the village, a warrior joined us to establish that we were visiting in peace and, once confirmed, a woman sang a song of welcome and offered us seating. Then the village elder gave an opening speech, after which we had to sing a song in Māori in support of him. Each of us was then greeted by other villagers with the *hongi*. This traditional form of greeting involves touching forehead to forehead which represents the exchange of knowledge, followed by the touching of nose to nose, which mingles the breath and makes two people one.

Finally, young people entertained us with gentle dancing and singing in the traditional manner, and then we European ladies were invited to join them, so as usual I was more than enthusiastic to join in. Next, the Māori men performed the *haka*, the traditional manner to show respect to adversaries. This they did by bending with their legs apart, slapping themselves, growling and poking out their tongues. After the performance, the European men were invited to join in and it was most amusing as, in their modern clothes and lack of experience, they certainly did not look frightening. It was then time to leave after a thoroughly delightful experience.

Norway, 2010

The world's northernmost ice hotel – the Sorrisniva Igloo Ice Hotel - is built entirely from ice every year and is open for up to 60 guests from January until April, when the average temperature is between four and seven degrees Celsius. Like many conventional hotels it had public lounges and a bar, both of which were decorated with ice sculptures carved by local artists, but it also included a chapel. The bedrooms were off along a corridor and each had a fabric curtain at the open entrance to the bedroom where the bed linen was to be a sleeping bag with blankets of reindeer furs. The bed was king size and deep.

Outside was a hot tub and all could be approached from a

warm large traditional wooden structured lodge which was in the shape of a *lavvu* tent. It was here that the toilets, showers, kitchen and small restaurant and, for me, a refuge were accommodated. On the evening of my stay I along with several other guests enjoyed a two-course dinner in the lodge where, for the main course, we were offered a choice of reindeer or salmon. I selected reindeer. Following dinner, we adjourned to the hotel bar to sit on the ice stools for a drink of bright blue vodka served in a "glass" of ice. Afterwards, those brave enough took a dip in the outside hot tub, but as this did not appeal, I returned to the lodge to consider my options.

To sleep in the hotel there were a number of situations which could prove unpleasant. Being in a sleeping bag my large snow boots would not fit into it. If I wanted to use the toilet I would need to get my boots on without touching any ice surface (which would be impossible), walk the corridor then an take an open pathway to get to the lodge. After this, I would of course then have to make the return journey. There were no lights as such, and it was a misty cold atmosphere. The lodge was to be empty of staff and the tour guide had also left. Thus, on balance, I felt that I would be in an unsecure cold place and plumped for sleeping on a bench seat in the lodge.

I was faintly amused as early on during the night, various guests sought the warmth and comfort of the lodge, so with all the comings and goings I really did not get much sleep. The next morning, staff arrived and we had a buffet breakfast before we carried out our chosen activities in our overtired state.

Being well wrapped up for the Arctic weather I visited the

Holmen Hundester Dog Sledging Centre, a vast area where wooden sledges were waiting and dozens of husky dogs were jumping, yapping and barking with excitement knowing that they would soon be pulling their passengers. Before the ride, the "Mushers" who trained and owned the dogs gave a talk about the care and dedication they gave to their animals, which was returned with total trust on both sides. Such training was for a March annual event called the *Finnmarksløpet* which is the longest in Europe. It lasts for over a week when both the dogs and Mushers need true stamina to compete in one of two races. One uses eight dogs for 600km and the other 12 dogs for 1000km. By the end of the talk, and having enjoyed hot refreshments and cake in our *lavvu*, I was raring to go. The sledge accommodated two seated, rug-wrapped people, one in the front of the sledge and the other at the rear. Behind me, the Musher stood guiding and encouraging his eight dogs to run at high speed. It was like a race, with each Musher trying to overtake the other. Whilst running, the dogs did not drop their speed as they licked the piled up snow on either side of the run. It ended all too soon after 20 minutes of high excitement and it was time to leave such inspiring, tough, handsome dogs and people.

From the centre I took the coach for a short journey to Boazo Sami Siida, a traditional reindeer herders' settlement. There, a herder explained how reindeer were herded and I was able to handle some of the tools and utensils which were used at the settlement. Some herders chanted Sami chants known as *joik* whilst others demonstrated lasso throwing. Meanwhile, the reindeer were nearby and smaller than those which Santa Clause seems to use! They seemed very calm and accepted the patting I gave them without moving away. Once again a *lavvu* was in use and an inside fire heated the coffee being offered. This was a day of hardy, caring people and beautiful animals.

Golden Oldies Living it Up in Paris, 2010

As two couples and two singles who had met on different cruises over three or four years, our group found that we had a lot in common: we were active, lively and well-informed; we enjoyed spirited conversations, food and a glass or two; and three of us smoked. By chance, we lived within driving distance of each other and all of this lay the foundations of our becoming firm friends and enjoying many outings together in the UK.

Over one of our lunches in my garden, and being adventurous, we decided to go over to Paris for a long weekend to enjoy a dinner sailing the Seine. Sightseeing on this occasion was not a priority as we had all been to Paris on many occasions. We met at St Pancras Station in high spirits to take the Eurostar and, as per usual, chatted and enjoyed some wine, and arrived at the Gare du Nord safely before taking a taxi to our hotel. We soon dressed for the occasion and enjoyed seeing Paris by night. The next day some of us had a look around a market and the side streets before meeting up for lunch. A French waiter was curious and expressed an interest in us and so I explained that we were OAPs let out once a year from our care homes to enjoy ourselves. I know it was naughty but what a story, and he believed it!

By the time we were travelling home, we were exhausted and had very little to say, which was the total opposite of how we had been when we left the UK at the beginning of our weekend. It was then that one of our number reminded us that we had 450 years between us, and we had to admit to the fact that we were no longer the travelling hippies we thought we were.

A Restaurant Story, London, 2011

With friends, we decided to book lunch at a West End Russian restaurant called Abracadabra so that one of our number could enjoy practising his Russian. The restaurant was large, opulent and impressive, with plenty of soft lights and plush red and silver decor. Much to our surprise we were the only diners and this remained so throughout the afternoon. The waiter was a Londoner, and apart from serving us, he enjoyed chatting about our venue as it was also a nightclub with a dance floor in the basement for which entrance was free to females, and there was an upper floor where they could relax. He also said that best tickets could always be obtained for top private clubs, venues and theatres.

The owner had made his fortune in the 1980s from those flocking across the Channel to purchase beer, wine, and spirits. He had bought a French restaurant but as it was not a success, and had changed it into one serving Russian cuisine. He also owned other nightclubs, bars and lap dancing clubs, and it so happened that he was there on the reception desk that afternoon. We were intrigued, especially as he had a brief chat with us as we left. Afterwards we enjoyed speculating about what we had been told, and were especially amused because none of us could remember anything we had had to eat or drink. Not until 2014 when the newspapers reported a murder did we realise that we had met the victim, the owner of the restaurant. He had been stabbed to death by his 45 year-old son. At his trial for manslaughter in 2015, it was said that his father had been a bully all his life and his son could stand it no longer. He was found guilty and jailed for 13 years.

It just goes to show, eating out can be an unexpected experience.

World Cruise, 2012

We were halfway through the journey from Sydney, Australia to Cairns when a passenger became dangerously ill and required immediate hospitalisation. To save his life, we were informed that a helicopter had been requested and was on its way to the ship to transport the patient to a hospital. We were asked to co-operate with the captain and crew by following their instructions and for our safety to either return to our cabins or to the ballroom, all of which were well away from any large plate glass windows. Any smaller windows were protected by the heavy closed curtains.

Meanwhile, the captain kept us informed as to the preparation onboard which was impressive as the officers and crew were obviously well-trained for their respective duties. All the furniture and electric bunting were removed from the back decks, the firefighting crew in their protective clothing were on alert as were the divers in their diving suits, and, armed with their walkie-talkies, other essential officers and crew were also in attendance. As the helicopter approached, the ship was manoeuvred into the best position for its personnel with a stretcher basket to be lowered onto the deck where the ship's doctor and nurses were then able to transfer the patient before he was winched up. Fortunately it was daylight and the weather was calm but even so, the whole operation still took some four hours. However, I was onboard on another similar occasion when the weather was really bad and it was not such an easy rescue, but was still successful.

Life at sea is never dull. One day on the cruise, we had just left Malaysia when the passengers were asked to gather and the Captain informed us that it was known that pirates from Somalia may be present in the area as we made our way to Ski Lanka. We were then introduced to a team of four armed Marines and two Royal Navy Officers who had boarded at our last port and were there to defend us and tell us what we should do if attacked. They had already put razor wire around the lower decks, fitted high pressure water cannons, and if the attack were to come at night, lights would be lowered and a huge searchlight used. In addition, the ship would go into full speed.

What to do in the event of pirates boarding the ship? An alarm would sound and the Captain would announce: "Piracy attack, take measures." We should go to non-glass areas as the pirates were rotten shots and glass could shatter, also the huge water steel doors would automatically close to frustrate the enemy. We then had a practice drill so that we would be prepared. After dinner, I went on deck whilst others were enjoying the entertainment, only to find the ship was virtually in total darkness. All the deck festoon lights were off - with one exception. Both the ship and sea were black and ominous and, for the first time, I saw the beauty of the constellations above. The ship was moving at high speed, and a crew member, without being obvious, checked with his torch that I was indeed a passenger. Sitting on the smoking deck, various people would arrive and no one would be able to see them, so we would all have to identify ourselves to any newcomers.

It was an interesting experience and I am pleased to say, we never saw a pirate!

Swimming with Stingrays, Antigua, 2012

My new – and thankfully docile – swimming partner

Transported by speedboat out to sea to an enclosed area and then in bathing suits, a lifejacket, snorkel and goggles, our brave group were told how to interact with the fish and how to avoid being attacked. Gingerly, with bare feet, I dismounted from steps into the sea, and as had been instructed, shuffled along the shallow water. This was essential, helping to ensure that I did not stand on one and be subjected to a potentially deadly barb attack. As they swam by, I fed them baby octopus, ensuring that the octopus was dangling from my fist with my thumb held protected inside. The stingrays would then glide to the food, and with a fast gulp snatch it and swallow it. No, not my thumb!

They were such beautiful, graceful creatures and they spent

the rest of the time swimming between people in their area. At the same time, I was able to stroke their backs which were as soft as silk and which they also seemed to enjoy. However, sometimes they came rather too close to an intimate part of the body thinking that it was food! At this point we had been urged not to make any movement but to freeze and they would move away and cause no harm. If one moved, the fish would think that it was at risk of losing its food and go for it with a quick strong suck. This would result in a nasty bruise and a bit of bleeding. The local guide also informed us that it would look rather like a hicky.

A great day out, but thankfully no love bite.

Mombasa, Kenya, 2012

I was sitting in the roadside backseat of the parked people carrier waiting for the arrival of other cruise passengers. The road was very busy with passing bicycles, cars, carts and pedestrians in colourful clothes. I mused that the sight would make an interesting photograph so I opened the adjacent small sliding window and pointed my camera in the forward direction.

Within moments a hand was all I saw as it snatched my camera! The hand belonged to a tall traditionally-dressed man who, unbelievably, did not change his slow walking pace as he casually continued walking away from the vehicle as if nothing had happened. What he had not known, was that the elasticated camera strap was around my wrist and so within seconds it had sprung back into my hand. The thief had to be admired as he showed no reaction and just continued on his way. On this occasion all I could do was to think: lucky me!

A Dead Sea Experience, 2012

Like so many, I was aware that the Dead Sea has the lowest, saltiest body of water in the world and contains a wealth of minerals. Evidently, its mud and waters are deemed extremely healthy for many physical and mental complaints and as a consequence, spas and hotels are nearby to accommodate guests. However, due to the water's composition, vegetation and living creatures are unable to survive. Thus, being in the area I just had to have another experience, not in an hotel, but to bathe in the sea. Prior to entering the sea with others, I was given some essential information. We were assured that sinking would be impossible; swimming could not be achieved but floating could for no more than 15 minutes; water must not enter the eyes or mouth; and afterwards, it was essential to soap all over and have a long shower.

By now I was feeling rather apprehensive but decided it would be a bit of an adventure. To enter the deep sea I stood with a queue of people in an open tunnel in the shallows which led into a square open cage situated in the deep sea area. From here, I had to slowly enter the open sea and then allow the legs to rise, and gently lean back. This was so frightening as I had no control whatsoever over my body. Panic made me want to swim, but this was quite impossible as the water would not allow me to be on my front. Within a very short time I decided that enough was enough and somehow floated to shore. This was not one of the most exciting moments of my life!

Madeira, 2019

On a Christmas cruise there was an excursion to Madeira to tour the island in a sidecar. As usual, I had to do something

I had not done before and added to which, it would be unlikely that I would get such an experience in the future.

The day arrived and on the dock side, three shiny motorcycles with their riders were waiting. I noted that one had a rather large paunch, another was overweight and the third looked younger, taller, slender and rather more professional in his riding gear. I was more than hopeful that he would be my driver. Unknowingly, I chose his vehicle. Hurrah! My fellow cruise traveller preferred to sit behind the driver as in her youth she had ridden as a passenger on her husband's bike, so I was assured of my place.

Our biker gave us helmets, and then I made a couple of ladylike attempts to clamber into the sidecar which was much lower and more awkward than I had anticipated. At last sitting on the hard seat and belted in, we were on our way with the cobbled road vibrating my rear end, the wind tearing into my face, and hanging onto the helmet which was rocking and rolling on my smaller head. Fortunately, the pillion rider indicated that I had to pull down the visor fitted to the top of the helmet which did overcome one problem, but the others remained. Nevertheless, the tour stops gave me some respite even though each time I took the helmet off my hairstyle was as flat as a pancake. Actually, I really enjoyed the tour and the ride itself was great fun. Mind you, getting out of the sidecar was not a simple feat but I truly felt like a with-it woman.

USA, 2019

A cruise to New York, calling in at Miami and Cape Canaveral, was hard to resist especially as my Canadian friends whom I had not seen for a number of years said that they would meet with me when the ship docked. Being Christmas time I invited them on board for the day in Miami and thought that as they loved Marks and Spencer's individual mince pies and Christmas puddings they could enjoy them with their meal on the 25th. Unbeknown to me, they had as a gift a special liqueur and a homemade key lime pie made especially by an American friend of theirs.

The only way to arrive into NYC – with a glass in hand

Meanwhile I was informed that US Customs banned food and drinks being taken off the ship, so when they arrived I said that their unexpected present could be unwrapped but then they would have to give them back. They too told me that the surprise pie and liqueur had also been banned from being brought onto the ship. We then spent some time trying to think how to overcome the problem with Customs. However, it was decided not to try to be clever as the outcome and potential consequences outweighed the enjoyment of the gifts.

The next day, the 24th, they drove to meet the ship in Cape Canaveral and gave me a tour in their luxurious golden Cadillac. As it was Christmas Eve the roads and area were deserted so we did not have to contend with much traffic. Afterwards they had arranged for us to have lunch at a nearby fresh fish restaurant. I was intrigued by a notice outside which refused entry to patrons with dogs in prams. My friends explained that such practice was common in America. The restaurant was buzzing with conversation, being full with friends and families dressed in various Christmas garbs enjoying the festivities. The menu was extensive, and I knew as soon as I saw freshly caught shark, that that had to be my choice. It was super, being tender and mild in taste.

Eventually, it was time to say goodbye – with an unexpected surprise. We parked way down in the semi-darkness in the terminus car park without another car in sight. Then out of the boot they produced plastic flutes, plates, forks and paper napkins. A bottle of liqueur was opened and a key lime pie sliced. We sat, enjoyed and laughed. I felt like singing *We Shall Overcome*, and when we parted I decided that this was certainly a memory to cherish forever.

Cotton Club, Harlem, NYC, 2020

While on the cruise, I was really excited to see that I could make an excursion to the famous Cotton Club which I had heard so much about over the years. To get in the mood, and in readiness for my latest adventure, I researched its history. In 1920, it was originally called the *Club De Luxe* and was a supper club on the first floor of a building in New York City. Owned by a heavyweight boxer, it became a legendary nightclub. However, in 1923 it was bought by a bootlegger and gangster upon his release from Sing Sing Correctional Facility. He then renamed it *The Cotton Club,* and numerous famous jazz singers performed there over the years, including Duke Ellington, Cab Calloway and Ella Fitzgerald. The Club finally closed in 1940, and it was not until the end of 1977 that it was reincarnated.

The evening arrived and I was dressed accordingly for such a special event and looking forward to an evening of jazz in a sophisticated, chic and glamorous venue. As it was Christmas time, New York was sparkling with festive decorations, brightly lit shop displays, plenty of people well wrapped against the cold and traffic jams throughout. Thus, our coach was the last to arrive.

The entrance to the club was very small, dingy, and not at all impressive. Inside it was low-ceilinged, small and very cramped, with long tables arranged in lines, whilst access to the chairs was an obstacle course. Once seated, I was virtually imprisoned. Those who had arrived earlier were seated around a tiny dance floor behind which was a small, low podium where the musicians were to play. Nevertheless, every part of the venue looked old, sad, tired and in need of an uplift and refit. Included in the price were two glasses of wine or beer. An tall, aged, stooping and rather grumpy waiter demanded our order and then, clearly not happy at having to serve about 90 tourists, simply ambled off. Just in case things got even stranger, I had ordered one glass of red and one of white, both of which proved to be undrinkable.

Finally, about five aged musicians arrived with two singers who were also a part of the entertainment. The first, a man, sang ballads, and he encouraged people to get up onto the postage size dance floor. The second performer was a mature lady looking dressed for the part, and absolutely superb at singing jazz. I felt that in her day she must have been a true professional singer and certainly the best experience of the whole evening. It really was a night to remember for all the wrong reasons, and sadly perhaps the biggest disappointment of my many travel experiences.

A Nightclub Dance, 2020

Over several cruises I got to know a youngish fellow passenger, Tony, who buzzed around the ship in his electric wheelchair. I really admired him, as he joined in many activities and excursions where, under certain situations such as the dance classes, he could discard his chair and wear metal leg braces and move with the aid of sticks. At the classes, the teacher would dance by holding him up and steady whilst keeping in time to the music, and using a limited step movement. I never saw him during his lessons but this came to light during my dance experience with him.

Two nights before I was to disembark, I attended the formal evening cocktail party and dinner dressed in an evening gown and the usual high heeled evening shoes. Afterwards, and towards the end of the evening, I went to the nightclub where I saw Tony, and not wishing to offend him, accepted his invitation to dance. I assisted him to get onto the nearby small dance floor but it was only then that I realised that I would have to support his weight and his heavy leg braces. Suddenly, the ship lurched and I tried to keep my balance whilst trying to prevent Tony from falling. I failed, and in doing so, fell backwards onto the floor, with him landing on top of me. It seemed as if everyone rushed to help him whilst leaving me to get to my feet unaided. The dance then continued with a member of the crew and myself jointly supporting Tony.

The next morning and to my horror, I found that from my waist down to my feet I was a mass of black and blue bruises, and so much so I could hardly walk. As I did not want to cause any embarrassment, I stayed in my cabin for most of the day until I could slowly get to the dining room by using a lift rather than taking the stairs which I had found impossible to use and negotiate due to the pain I was experiencing.

Fortunately, the following day was when I was to disembark, and by then the pain was less severe and I could cope with my hand luggage. However, I learned yet another lesson, that in the future, to follow my head rather than my heart.

16 AFTERWORD

My enthusiasm following my retirement over preserving my work for whatever historical interest it might hold was one thing, but it was a whole different story when it came to a pile of VHS and Betamax tapes of my various TV appearances that I managed to unearth. I was blissfully unaware that YouTube had been thrust upon the world in 2005. Four years later – without realising the consequences – I just happened to mention in passing to two friends, Peter (whom I knew from *Weekend Listener*) and Matt, that these old recordings were quietly rotting away in an old wooden chest. So when they asked to view them, and then insisted that we set up a channel to showcase them, I was highly dubious at the prospect! I couldn't imagine why anyone would want to watch them.

It took a little bit of time and gentle persuasion until my YouTube channel was born in January 2010. Around that time, I was also working with a local museum. I found myself being invited to talk to various groups to give a presentation I had developed with old-fashioned 35mm slides to tell the past story of electrical goods in the home. For schoolchildren, I had opted to call myself the Appliance Historian. So this was the name we adopted for my new channel. VHS players had long been superseded, but luckily with the aid of an old video machine, the tapes were pretty straightforward to digitise and upload – not by me, I hasten to add!

But what to do with the Betamax recordings? Little did I

know in 1984 when I set my home video to record my breakfast appearances on TV-AM that Betamax was about to lose the videotape format war. Luckily, Peter was able to contact our friend Mike, who worked his magic, and my early morning appearances were saved for the nation!

Needless to say that I was amazed when our YouTube viewing figures started creeping up. As I write in 2021, we've just broken the 200,000 views barrier. Little did I realise what was in store, when I had set my domestic recorder merely for my own records, decades earlier! It is so delightful that viewers take the time and trouble to watch and send a message or a 'Like' in response to one of my old videos. But if ever I take an occasional peek at my TV past, my reaction is: is that really me?!

Several friends have asked how I have managed to remember so many events. I find it difficult to find an explanation but I have always enjoyed both world and family history, whether in the verbal or written form. Added to which, my mother was a great raconteur and an avid diary writer, whilst my parents loved people of any age, and all had stories to tell. Thus, without being aware, I was fuelled throughout my youth, and as a result loved to write poetry, kept a diary, and eventually wrote the many books, resources and articles referenced in this book.

Over the years, I tended to remember events and often wrote long descriptive diaries many of which I illustrated with photographs. Today, in addition, and to ensure accuracy of dates or my descriptions etc., I turn to the Internet for verification. As I can only use one finger on each hand, fast and accurate typing is not my forte. Fortunately, with the wonderful world of technology, I chat randomly to the computer dictation tool and then spend time rewriting and editing the text.

I didn't really think I was doing anything special. I was really just doing my job. Like my mother when she was in service, I was fulfilling my duties. I didn't appreciate the value of what I was doing at the time. Now, looking back, I realise what influence I had and what I was achieving in the industry. At no point in my life or career did I think that I would be sitting here all these years later with my YouTube channel and its back catalogue of my old TV and radio appearances, preserved for posterity in the social media age. I add to it every now and then when long-unseen items resurface, and I'm amazed and delighted in equal measure that the things that we post still seem in some way to strike a chord with a modern audience.

I think in many ways, in spite of changes in technology, society and behaviours, that what makes people tick hasn't really changed that much. Although we might take electricity for granted, the things it does, powers and enables us to do continue to fascinate and inspire us. People still need to eat, they still need to cook their food and heat their homes and they still need to make sensible purchasing decisions based on their requirements and budget. It was a privilege to be part of helping to promote effective and safe use of electricity in the home and to enable others to discover the wonders of its potential. As I sit here, I can't help but imagine what the teenage girl in the showroom a lifetime ago would have made of all of the miracles electricity brings into our contemporary lives day in, day out.

Jenny Webb
September 2021

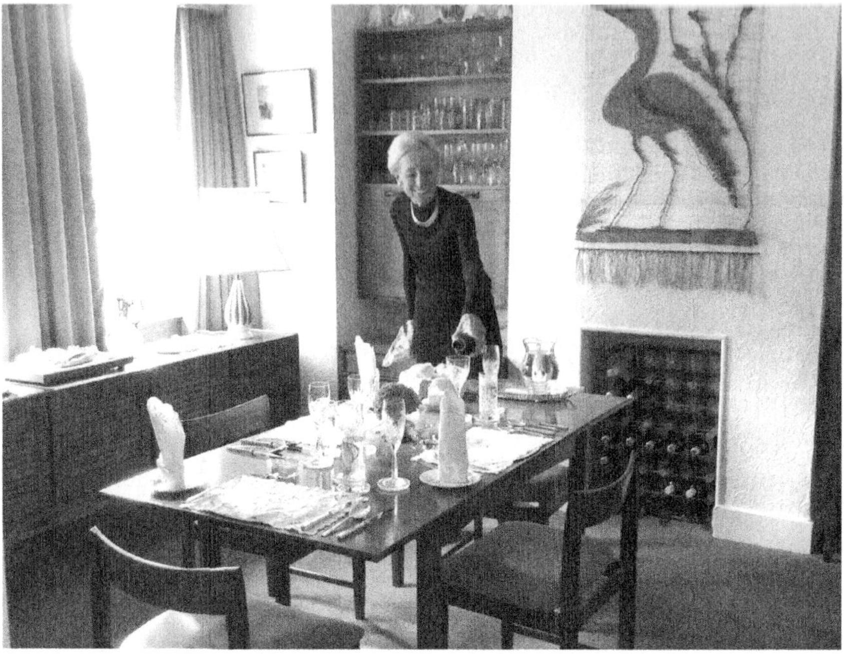

17 BIBLIOGRAPHY

Poetry published in two anthologies: *Poetry Today 1972* and in *Spring Poems 72* (Regency Press, 1972)

Jenny Webb's Mixer and Blender Book (Woodhead Faulkner, 1977)

Microwave - The Cooking Revolution (Forbes, 1977)

The Microwave Cookbook (Forbes, 1978)

Microwave Cooking at Home authored jointly with Gwen Conacher (Electricity Council, 1980)

The Safety and Performance of Domestic Electrical Appliances (British Standards Institution, 1982)

The Marks and Spencer Book of Microwave Cooking (Octopus, 1983). Published in French as *Les Micro-ondes*

Two-Way Cookbook authored jointly with Marguerite Patten (BEA Publishers, 1984)

Menus for the Microwave Hostess as Marie Emmerson (Octopus, 1986)

Marks and Spencer Microwave Entertaining as Marie Emmerson (Octopus, 1986). Published in French as *Les Micro-ondes pour Reçevoir* (Gründ, 1987)

The Good Housekeeping Microwave Cooking Course as Marie Emmerson (Ebury Press, 1986)

The Farmhouse Microwave Cookbook authored jointly with Grace Mulligan (Yorkshire TV, 1986)

Cooking for Today - Microwave Entertaining as Marie Emmerson (Hamlyn, 1988)

The Farmhouse Kitchen Freezer and Microwave Cookbook as Marie Emmerson (Yorkshire TV Enterprises, 1989)

Freeze and Microwave - Food for Thought (Yorkshire TV Enterprises, 1991). Also published on audio cassette by the Electricity Association.

The Kitchen Gadget Book authored jointly with Dianne Page and Annette Yates (Clarion, 1997)

The Fan Oven Book (Rightway Books, 2001)

Jenny Webb's Talking Microwave Recipes (Cobalt Systems Ltd - CD and cassette)